A DEGREE OF SWING

Lessons in the facts of life; Leicester 1958–64

COLIN MILLER

A DEGREE OF SWING

Lessons in the facts of life; Leicester 1958–64

To Garfield

First published in Great Britain in 2012 by The Derby Books Publishing Company Limited, 3 The Parker Centre, Derby, DE21 4SZ.

This paperback edition published in Great Britain in 2013 by DB Publishing an imprint of JMD Media Ltd.

ISBN 978-1-78091-009-3
Printed and bound by Copytech (UK) Ltd, Peterborough

CONTENTS

ACKNOWLEDGEMENTS

This book describes my experiences as a young man while studying at Leicester University between 1958 and 1964, based mainly on my memories of that time. I have tried to be as accurate as possible in describing the changes and events that occurred so many years ago, but memories are not always reliable and can fade over time. So I must apologise for any factual errors that I may inadvertently have made. In order to supplement my recollections I have referred to contemporary written sources, including editions of the *Leicester Mercury* and the Leicester University Students' newspaper *Ripple*, as well as to the memories of my friends and student colleagues. I feel that the resulting book is a fair and accurate account of my time in Leicester and reflects the many issues, problems and challenges that faced not only me but most of my generation on reaching adulthood in the early years of the 1960s. It also describes the changes that were taking place in young people's opinions and tastes, especially in music and fashion, and the influence those changes had on the everyday lives of ordinary young men and women. I have described my thoughts and views as honestly as I can and have tried not to include material that would embarrass or offend any of my contemporaries. I have used full names only for those individuals whose names are either already in the public domain or who are fully aware of the contents of this book. All interpretations of events and any opinions expressed in the text are those of the author.

Writing the book has given me immense pleasure, but it would not have been possible without the encouragement and help that I received from many individuals and organisations. I wish to thank my wife, Dr Celia Miller, for her patience, encouragement and practical assistance with the text, and my many friends for sharing their personal experiences with me. My thanks go to my student musician friends for the considerable assistance given to me while I was producing this volume, especially Russ Dear, Eric Flitney and Trevor Smith from the Leicester University rock band, *Aztec and the Incas*. A special mention is due to Rod (*Aztec*) Davies for his interest and help and for allowing me to use many illustrations taken from his collection of contemporary photographs. Writing this book has enabled me to meet again with many friends from the past, although others remain only as memories. Regrettably, some are no longer with us, including Alan Makin, founder member of the group *Johnny Angel and the Mystics.* I am most grateful for the help given to me during my research by the staff of the Leicester University Library, especially the members of the Special

Collections Department; the staff at the Leicester, Leicestershire and Rutland Record Office; Alex Cave, Leicester University Archivist and Lynda Smart from the Leicester Mercury Media Group. I must thank Laura Smith and her colleagues at the Derby Book Publishing Company for the valuable assistance and advice offered during the production of this book.

My thanks go also to the individuals and organisations that have permitted me to use material derived from their albums and archives. I have made every effort to identify and contact all current copyright owners for their permission to reproduce the photographs and illustrations contained in this volume, but in some cases this proved impossible. In those instances I have attributed the images to the current owners. Unattributed illustrations are drawn from the author's personal collection. Among these are photographs of Leicester taken by Valentine & Sons Ltd of Dundee (currently in the possession of the University of St Andrews Library) and A.W. Holmes & Sons of Leicester. If I have omitted any person or organisation from the following list, I apologise and suggest that they contact me immediately through the publisher so that a full and correct acknowledgement can be given in any future reprint.

My thanks go to Kevin Shepherdson, manager of the Old Horse public house in Leicester; Rodney Davies; Russ Dear; Richard Tacon of Rollesby; the Leicester, Leicestershire and Rutland Record Office; the Leicester Mercury Media Group; Professor Stephen Brown at De Montfort University, Leicester; Dr Aubrey Stewart, archivist at the Leicester Royal Infirmary Hospital Museum and Alex Cave at the Leicester University Archives Department for their permission to use photographs and illustrations taken from their collections.

Colin Miller
February 2012

CHAPTER 1

AN UNEXPECTED OPPORTUNITY

Friday 22 August 1958 was the day that my life changed. It was the day when the Advanced level results for the General Certificate of Education were declared. When I returned home for tea from a long day assisting with the corn harvest on my friend Richard's father's farm, my nervous parents pointed apprehensively towards our fireplace. There, propped up behind the coronation mug on the mantelshelf, was the tell-tale, self-addressed brown envelope that I had left in the secretary's office at Great Yarmouth Grammar School on the last day of the summer term. The day that I had assumed was to be my final day at the grammar school before beginning to train as a Customs and Excise officer in Essex. Not that I was particularly optimistic or keen to open that letter, or even to discover its contents as both the headmaster and my sixth form tutor had already told me that I was unlikely to obtain any passes at this level and considered that I had neither the maturity nor the intellect necessary for progressing on to university. In their considered opinion it would be more appropriate for me to train as a primary school teacher or to join a branch of the civil service as a clerical officer.

So it was with some apprehension that I opened the envelope and read aloud the typewritten note inside. 'University of Cambridge Local Examinations Syndicate, General Certificate of Education, Colin R Miller, Mathematics, Advanced level pass, grade 2; Further Mathematics, Advanced level pass, grade 3; Physics, pass at Ordinary level'. 'Is that good?' asked mother. The results were indeed good, far better than I had been led to expect, and, as a consequence, were welcomed with rather mixed feelings; feelings of both delight and frustration. Delight at my obvious success despite the poor physics result (the physics teacher and I never did get on) and frustration that those results did indeed give me the qualifications necessary for a university education, an education that I had been persuaded to believe was beyond my capability. This was not the first time that my abilities had been underestimated by some of the teaching staff at Great Yarmouth Grammar School. Perhaps their views were inevitable, coloured by unconscious prejudices surrounding the small but rapidly expanding group of working-class boys and girls who were benefitting from the provisions of the 1944 Education Act and a grammar school education that had been unachievable for most of our parents.

I was born on 5 August 1940 at Rollesby, a small Broadland village in the county of

Norfolk, eight miles west of the seaside town of Great Yarmouth and 16 miles north-east of Norwich, where I lived with my parents, Raymond and Gertrude Miller, in a small semi-detached house that they rented from a neighbouring farmer. Our simple accommodation consisted of two reception rooms (a living room and a front room), a scullery, two double bedrooms and a box room which, although small, doubled as my bedroom and my study. We had neither an upstairs bathroom nor an indoor toilet, and all our fresh water was obtained from a single cold water tap in the scullery. My father was a skilful bricklayer and plasterer, and took great pride in his work. Often on a Sunday, mother and I were driven in my father's ancient car to inspect his latest building project, where he proudly boasted that 'This will still be here long after I am dead and gone'. For most of her life my mother had no full-time occupation. Like most working-class women of the time, she considered that her primary function was to look after the house and her family, and she was content not to seek regular paid employment. I was so used to being looked after by my mother that, when I eventually left home at the age of 19, I was totally unprepared for living independently on my own. To help with the family budget, she occasionally took seasonal part-time labouring work in the fields and market gardens of Rollesby, and as a Saturday cleaner at a riverside boatyard in the neighbouring village of Martham.

In the late 1950s, grammar school education was still dominated by staff and students from middle-class backgrounds, with a culture derived mainly from middle-

Rollesby, a quiet Norfolk village where I lived with my parents in the semi-detached house on the right. (R. Tacon)

class traditions, attitudes and values. My own cultural background was, inevitably, that of a working-class country boy – not the profile of the stereotypically successful 1950s grammar school pupil. I much preferred listening to Buddy Holly and Elvis Presley than to Beethoven and Elgar, and I had little understanding or appreciation for classical music, ballet or the theatre. I read non-fiction rather than fiction, and my knowledge of English literature was derived almost exclusively from film adaptations that I had seen at the cinema. I enjoyed practical subjects, most forms of sport and, being country born, I had a hands-on practical experience of nature.

A lengthy discussion with my parents persuaded me to abandon any thoughts of joining Customs and Excise and to consider applying for admission to a university. As by that time it was far too late to apply for the coming October, the headmaster suggested that I might benefit both personally and academically from a further year of study in the sixth form and so it was that I returned unexpectedly to Great Yarmouth Grammar School in September 1958. Eventually, I was encouraged to request prospectuses and application forms from a number of universities and to apply for selected courses at a minimum of three of them. After some discussion with my parents, I applied for entry to study for a degree in mathematics at the universities of Leicester, Hull and Nottingham, a choice that demonstrated my innate lack of self-confidence all too clearly because not only were they the closest universities to my home, they were also easily accessible by train. Until that time, I had very little personal experience of the world beyond a 20-mile radius of Great Yarmouth.

By the end of October, I had received replies from all three universities. At Nottingham and Hull I was immediately offered a place to study mathematics based on my A level results of the previous summer. Leicester, however, invited me to attend an interview at the university at 3pm on Wednesday 1 November 1958. As Leicester University was my first choice, I duly accepted. At the time, Leicester London Road Station was one of the stops on a direct rail route from Great Yarmouth Beach Station to Birmingham, originally a main line route of the Midland and Great Northern Railway. It was a convenient route for me as I could board the train at Martham Station, a stop on the route a mere mile away from my Norfolk home. Although this was the real reason for preferring Leicester, I tried to convince my school colleagues that my choice was based primarily on the high proportion of female students currently studying at the university. Leicester University selected proportionately more female students than most other universities of the late 1950s. Nevertheless, women students were still a minority group everywhere.

When the day of the interview finally arrived, I walked to Martham Station and boarded the early morning steam train from Great Yarmouth to Birmingham clutching my return ticket to Leicester in one hand and my school briefcase in the other. Dressed in my best school uniform, specially cleaned for the occasion, I was as presentable as mother could make me. I was not too happy wearing school clothes for the interview but mother had vetoed my attempt to travel in the jazzy blue and red checked suit that I normally wore for dances. In my pocket I had a one pound note for food and accommodation should I not be able to catch the last train back to Great Yarmouth, and in my briefcase were the letter of invitation from the university, a flannel, a bar of soap, my toothbrush and toothpaste, and two rounds of cheese and tomato sandwiches wrapped in greaseproof paper for my lunch. I was obsessed by steam trains but had never travelled more than 10 miles on one, so the journey was a long-anticipated adventure. I spent most of the time staring out of the carriage window at the passing countryside enjoying the changing scenery. Sadly, the three hour journey seemed to be over in no time and I arrived at Leicester's London Road Station all too soon.

Luckily, I discovered from a luggage porter that the university was not too far from the station. As I had plenty of time to spare, I ambled in the direction of the campus looking in every shop widow before resting on a bench in the nearby Victoria Park to eat my sandwiches. Arriving at the university, I reported to the reception desk and was

The first thing I saw as I left the station was a student cycling down London Road with his university scarf flapping in the breeze. 'That could be me', I thought.

led to a row of chairs outside the room where the interview was to take place. The interviews were running late and I was not called into the interview room until well after 4pm. Putting on my best accent, I proceeded to answer the questions posed by my interviewer. Mother had impressed on me the need to speak in proper BBC English, a difficult task for someone who had spent all his life in rural Norfolk. My attempts failed miserably, as my interviewer commented that 'It is nice to meet someone who is not ashamed of his broad regional accent'. From that moment, I ceased trying to hide my Norfolk brogue, but soon discovered that not everyone at the university appreciated a regional accent.

The sore finger of speech protrudes

In an age characterised by unlovely uniformity, the lack of an educated accent here in Leicester comes as a pleasant surprise. One stands in the refectory queue at midday suffering the harangues of a thousand regional nuances, a cavalcade of dialects, aptly, overtly manipulated. The Cockney tongue prods the atmosphere, it's starkness a Stepney Green in the Percy Gee; at coffee sipping under the aroma of a Wigan slang ignoring and blatant, intent on its tone as it discusses problems of Sociology. And from the debating floor the drawling Yorkshire man curls his conversation, content in its incoherence. You may think me a prig. You may think that our state grammar schools have more important items on their curriculum than the cultivation of a Public School drawl; that πR^2 comes before an English sentence designed to convey delicate thoughts with clarity and charm. Nevertheless we dwell in a fraternity glistening with intellects, brimming with 'A' levels and English 'O', and yet our groups are often indistinguishable from a meeting of the executive of a Leicester Trade Union. What is to me most irritating is the invested pride these fools take in not only shouting their parts, but the obvious way they identify themselves. Italian shoes, pink shirts and the corresponding uniform of the 'Ted'. Let them be proud of their artisan parentage by all means, but let them keep their native habits, dress and slang to their vacation sojourns.

Leicester Diary, *Ripple*, 14 November 1960

During the interview I was asked about my financial circumstances and whether I would like to sit an entrance examination in the coming January for a bursary to supplement my grant. Naturally I agreed, which appeared to please my interviewer. At the end of our time together he asked how I intended to return home to Norfolk. 'By train', I said, but indicated that my journey might now be in the morning as the last train had probably already left Leicester. Enquiring where I intended to stay, I replied that I had seen a YMCA hostel close to the park and hoped to find a bed there for the night. This amused my interviewer, who suggested that I would enjoy my stay there as it was actually a YWCA, a hostel for young women and not for men. Sensing my inexperience in these matters, he took pity on me and immediately telephoned the warden of Beaumont Hall, a men's hall of residence belonging to the university, and arranged for me to spend the night there in a room set aside for guests. My brief but extremely comfortable overnight stay convinced me that Leicester was my first choice of university and a place in Beaumont Hall was my first choice of residence.

My destiny was decided two weeks later when I received a letter offering me a place on the university's BSc Special Mathematics course subject to three grade 3 passes at A level in the coming July examinations, or a place on the new modular BSc General Science degree with Pure Mathematics as a main subject unconditionally based on my two existing A level passes. Having no confidence at all in my ability to pass Physics at that level, I immediately wrote back accepting the latter offer. The letter also included an invitation to sit the examination for a bursary in early January, during the university's Christmas vacation. This involved a one or two-night stay in Leicester for those candidates who were travelling from a distance.

Every time I walked through Victoria Park to the university, I passed Leicester's impressive War Memorial.

College Hall, the residence for women students where I stayed while unsuccessfully sitting the examinations for an entrance scholarship. (Leicester Mercury Media Group)

So for the second time in two months, I found myself travelling by train to Leicester, walking up the hill, through the park, past the city's impressive War Memorial and on to the university. Fortunately I had managed to persuade my mother that casual clothes were the order of the day and so I was not subjected to the embarrassment of wearing my school uniform. For the duration of my stay I was allocated a room in a drab two-storey accommodation block located on the main campus, called College Hall, which normally served as a women's hall of residence during term time. To my great surprise and excitement, at the introductory meeting on the first evening I discovered that, of the 20 or more other candidates residing at the hall, at least half were women. I eventually discovered that the male candidates were allocated rooms on the ground floor while the women had been given rooms on the first, although this segregation appeared not to be strictly supervised. On each floor there was a kitchen, washroom and toilet block, while our main meals were taken in the dining room of an adjacent building – a building that I eventually came to know affectionately as the Percy Gee. At the introductory meeting we were told about the procedures for the two test papers to be taken the next day, one in the morning and one in the afternoon, as well as information about the city of Leicester and its facilities, which we were encouraged to explore in the spare time available to us.

The presence of young women gave added spice to this suggestion. Despite having had a steady girlfriend for well over a year, I was still sexually inexperienced. Opportunities to improve on my experience were limited and even when they did arise, the restraining hand of common sense normally called a halt long before the point of no return was reached. But here in Leicester, we were men and women brought together in a strange place and far away from the constraints of home and the presence of a regular girl or boyfriend. It was a commonly-held belief among my male contemporaries that young women away from their home environment lost all inhibitions regarding sex. This was one of the many misconceptions held by imaginative young men who spent most of their time segregated in a school for boys and were inexperienced in the ways of women. Our misconceptions were undoubtedly derived from the abandoned behaviour of some young people when they were staying in Great Yarmouth for their summer holidays. Nevertheless, I had been presented with an opportunity to test this belief and, possibly, to explore experiences that had, as yet, not been mine to savour.

So, after the examinations were over, I joined forces with another young man whose thought processes were as misguided as my own and together we invited two young Welsh women to accompany us in an exploration of Leicester on the second evening of our stay. After a pleasant evening watching a film from the back row seats of a city centre cinema, during which the young women failed to show any signs of lost inhibitions, we returned to hall and said good night, taking care to indicate the location of our bedrooms, albeit with little hope of success. Unfortunately, it was not the knock of a female hand on my door that awoke me in the night, but the agony of violent stomach cramps and the sense of an impending disastrous event. Running quickly to the toilet block, I joined a queue of other young men who had been similarly afflicted by a mild case of food poisoning – not an uncommon experience for university students as I later discovered. The situation was the same with the female residents upstairs, including my two new Welsh friends. Fortunately for me, the carriages on the return train home had both a corridor and a toilet. The examinations were also a great disappointment, because I had barely understood most of the questions and, unsurprisingly, I was not awarded the further financial bonus of a bursary.

Thirty girls poisoned

On Thursday 21st January, College Hall echoed with groaning. About thirty girls in this part of Women's Hall were suffering from a mysterious stomach ailment. Detailed investigations revealed that the sufferers had all been to early supper. It is suspected that meat served at supper was the cause of a minor bout of food poisoning.

Ripple, 6 February 1960

In no time at all, my extra year at school was over. My second take of the A level examinations had gone reasonably well and were less stressful than those of the previous year, undoubtedly because I was better prepared and my entry into the General Science course at Leicester was not dependent upon the results. The last day of term, my final day as a schoolboy, saw the usual idiotic and juvenile high jinks. A final lunchtime spent in the bar of a local public house resulted in someone removing the wheels from a master's car and placing them on the roof of the sixth form annex. This 'joke' was not entirely appreciated by either the headmaster or the car's owner. When the A level results were finally declared, I had not only passed Mathematics and Further Mathematics with exactly the same grades that I had received the previous year but I had also passed Physics at grade 3. If I had only had the confidence, those results would have qualified me for entry into Leicester's Special Mathematics course, but I was quite content to continue on the apparently less demanding General Science course. A course entitled Special Mathematics could prove very challenging and the experience of the January bursary examinations demonstrated clearly that my knowledge of mathematics was limited.

As soon as I had informed the university of my A level results, I received a letter confirming that I had been allocated a residential place in Beaumont Hall together with a list of books to read in preparation for student life. I was surprised to see that most of these recommended books were works of fiction written by well-known authors of English literature. What these had to do with mathematics I was not at all sure. I tried reading one or two from the list but quickly gave up, preferring to read my choice of biographies of famous scientists, books on astronomy and accounts of military campaigns in the Korean and Second World wars. I was also required to undertake a radiography examination to ensure that my lungs were free from tuberculosis.

Many of my sixth form friends were similarly in limbo. Tim was waiting to begin a chemistry degree at Manchester University, Bill was joining the army with the intention of becoming an officer, Henry was reading mathematics at Nottingham, Roy was taking dentistry at Leeds and most of the others were soon to leave for various destinations all over the country. Together we spent most of our spare time talking and drinking espresso in a local coffee bar. Regrettably, our impending departures were exerting great pressures on some of our personal relationships. Unlike many of my village friends, most of who were now at work, we were discouraged by our parents and teachers from becoming too attached to a member of the opposite sex. In their opinion, it was inevitable that regular separations and a three-year wait before a real commitment was possible would be too great a strain on any teenage relationship, as proved to be the case with my own. My first serious girlfriend and I parted one month before I left for Leicester. For some individuals the thought of an impending separation, even if it was only temporary, gave their relationships an increased intensity with the potential for an unwanted outcome. Of those relationships that did survive the initial parting, many eventually drifted apart as the temptations of university life, freedom from the restraints of home and long periods of separation caused inevitable and irretrievable damage. It seemed that absence rarely made the heart grow fonder in most of our cases.

Chapter 2

A resident in Southmeade House

Friday 25 September 1959, the date for my departure from Rollesby and the start of my new life as a university student, finally arrived. My new crimson trunk had been collected on the previous day by a van from British Rail and was, hopefully, in transit to Beaumont Hall in Leicester. Before leaving home I loaned my record player to my mother and divided my pop music collection between her and my cousin Stephanie, under the misguided impression that rock 'n' roll music was considered to be non-U for university students. I bade a sad goodbye to my favourite record purchases of that year – Marty Wilde's recording of *Endless Sleep*, Ricky Nelson's *Poor Little Fool*, *When* by The Kalin Twins, Jerry Keller's *Here Comes Summer* and many others. On the other hand, my jazz records had been carefully packed in my trunk and accompanied me on my journey to Leicester. After consuming a breakfast of two shredded wheat biscuits in warm milk, carefully avoiding the skin that always formed on the top of the milk, I travelled with my parents to Vauxhall Station in Great Yarmouth to catch the 9.20am train to Leicester. Unfortunately, the direct route to Birmingham via Leicester from Great Yarmouth's Beach Station had just been axed as a result of cuts in services by British Rail and the journey now involved changes at Norwich and Ely. Trying hard not to be observed by the other departing students waiting nearby on the platform, I kissed my tearful mother goodbye and shook hands with my father before boarding the train. 'Work hard and don't get up to any mischief', was their parting advice.

As the train slowly steamed out of the station, I leaned out of the carriage window and waved enthusiastically through the billowing smoke until they were well out of sight. My life was about to change and their world and mine would be different from now on. As an only child, I had been their prime concern for the last 19 years and my departure would leave a void in their daily lives, especially for my mother. For my part, I was sad to leave the home and the village that I loved so much, but, at the same time, I was excited, apprehensive and a tiny bit scared of what lay ahead. I was accompanied on my journey to Leicester by Ray, a former colleague from school who was in his second year as a student studying physics. As we discussed the course that I was about to undertake, I became alarmed when he said that physics was the most difficult and demanding subject that the university offered. I was intending to take physics as a subsidiary subject and, remembering my past problems with it, I immediately resolved

Living at Beaumont Hall was a luxury beyond my wildest dreams. (Leicester Mercury Media Group)

to register for an alternative topic. When we arrived at Leicester we shared a taxi to Stoughton Drive South, where I reported to the reception at Beaumont Hall and Ray to Shirley Hall, just around the corner in nearby Manor Road.

On my arrival at Beaumont Hall, I was checked off a list by a receptionist and informed that I had been allocated a place in Southmeade House, an annexe of Beaumont Hall 100 yards further along Stoughton Drive, where I was to share a room with two other first year students. Both Beaumont and Southmeade were impressive buildings, especially to someone who had lived all his life in a small semi-detached house in rural Norfolk. Set in a leafy suburb of tree-lined roads and large houses with vast ornamental gardens, both buildings were erected in the early 1900s for a well-to-do hosiery manufacturer. Beaumont was acquired by the university in 1947 for use as a men's hall of residence, together with two other houses, Hastings and Shirley. Southmeade was bought and added to the Beaumont complex in 1956. With the exception of the construction of a kitchen and a large dining hall at Beaumont, both buildings were very little altered from their original designs. The grounds were immaculately kept and formed part of Leicester University's famous Botanic Gardens.

At Southmeade, I was ushered through the main entrance lobby into a long wood-panelled corridor with three rooms to the left: the original study, lounge and dining room, which had been converted into student accommodation. To the right of the corridor were a toilet and washroom, an ornamental wooden stairway to the first floor and windows looking out onto the front courtyard. At the far end of the corridor was the kitchen, with a staircase down to the cellar. The first floor consisted of a large bathroom, the main bedroom, which was used as accommodation for a postgraduate research student, and three or more smaller rooms that were occupied by second year students. The ground floor rooms had all been allocated to new students: Tony and Jim in the former study, Roger, David and me in the former lounge, and three botanists sharing the former dining room. A door from the first floor corridor led onto a narrow and precarious roof terrace where we spent many happy hours in the summer term revising for our examinations and peering over the fence at the sunbathing female residents of the Knoll, a large house belonging to the Fox family, the makers of Glacier Mints. Breakfast and evening meals were served in the dining hall at Beaumont every day, together with lunch on Saturdays and Sundays, all part of the residential package. After termly hall fees were deducted from my maintenance grant, the result of a scholarship awarded to me by the Norfolk Education Committee, I had about £30 left to buy books and stationary, and to cover all my daily expenses and entertainment for the rest of the term, approximately £3 a week.

In the lounge, I was introduced to my two new room-mates. Roger, a tall fair haired young man, who was always immaculately dressed every day in a dark suit, white shirt and tie, and highly polished black shoes, came from Windsor and David, a curly-haired, jolly character, originated from somewhere in Essex. Each of us was provided with a bed, a wardrobe, a chest of drawers, a stick backed chair and a desk, while the centre of the room boasted a low circular coffee table with three armchairs arranged around it. Set into the main wall was a large decorative stone fireplace and two wood-panelled side walls with connecting doors separated our lounge from the study and dining room. Along the fourth wall, an ornamental bay consisting of three large floor-to-ceiling sash-windows looked out over a terrace towards the botanic gardens.

Two female housekeepers looked after the house and the students. They cleaned our rooms, changed our bedding on a Friday, organised our laundry and set out and washed up our supper time crockery. Our only responsibilities were to make our beds every day and to iron our clothes which, in my case, proved to be a great mistake as I had never ironed before and I regularly scorched my shirt collars and tails as a result. Women visitors were permitted from 2pm until 10pm on Wednesdays, Saturdays and Sundays, and were to be entertained only in the Junior Common Room of the main Beaumont Hall building. Women were not allowed in any of the student rooms and all the outside doors were religiously locked at 11 o'clock in the evening. Any student

Southmeade House, where I shared a ground floor room with two other students. (Leicester University Archives)

staying out later than 11pm had to apply for a key. Unfortunately, my bed was against one of the windows in our ground floor accommodation and I was frequently woken late at night to admit returning students who had been locked out.

At dinner on the first evening we were addressed by the warden, Mr Bishop, an erudite character who looked and sounded exactly like the bearded actor James Robertson Justice. In his welcoming speech he extolled the virtues of life in hall and warned us strongly against bad behaviour. The dining hall was set out in rows of long refectory tables with benches on either side and on a raised stage was the high table where Mr Bishop sat centrally on a throne-like chair, flanked on each side by gowned members of staff and other important guests. Plated meals were collected by the resident students from a serving area while potatoes and vegetables were placed on the tables in large glass bowls. That evening, I was introduced for the first time to the joys of cauliflower cheese, a relatively simple dish that, surprisingly, did not feature at all in my mother's culinary repertoire. After dinner, five of us decided to explore the neighbouring village of Oadby where we each drank five pints of Mitchell and Butler's best bitter at the White Horse Inn and, being unused to such quantities, discovered that an excess of beer had a disastrous effect on cauliflower cheese. My first night in Leicester was spent staring at the bottom of a toilet bowl.

Beaumont Hall was located among the tree-lined lanes of Oadby, an unexpectedly quiet and leafy setting for a university men's hall of residence.

Despite the clear advantages of life in Beaumont Hall: the splendid accommodation that was far more lavish than anything that I had ever experienced before and the mothering of two hard-working and attentive housekeepers, there were also many disadvantages. The hall was on the outskirts of the city, some distance from the main university campus with its lecture rooms, library and entertainment facilities, and even

further from the attractions of Leicester's city centre. To walk to the university took at least 45 minutes, a route march often undertaken out of necessity when money was short. Needless to say, my first letter home contained a request for my parents to send me my bicycle so that I could join the long chain of cyclists making the morning ride into the university. Evening meals were often missed in order to save the long journey from the university to hall

During World War One, the Fielding Johnson served as the 5th Northern General Hospital for injured soldiers from the front.

for dinner and back again to the university or city centre for night-time entertainments. Whether it was deliberate or not, we were also located well away from the university's women's halls of residence.

Monday 28 September 1959 was registration day at the main campus and the first day of Freshers' Week, which consisted largely of one day spent standing in queues to sign up for courses followed by four days of coffee drinking, making new friends and being coerced into joining various clubs and societies. Leicester University, established in 1921 as a university college of London, became a university in its own right when it was granted a charter in May 1957. The campus, though small, was sufficient at the time to cater for its 800 or more students. The main building was a long, Victorian, three-storied barrack-like construction of grey stone which had previously been used as a mental asylum and then as a hospital for World War One casualties, re-named the Fielding Johnson Building in honour of the Leicester clothing manufacturer who had bought it in 1921 to house the proposed university college. Immediately in front of this building was a narrow roadway and beyond that a large lawn that sloped down to a high wall running along the main University Road. To one side of the lawn was the relatively

During Freshers' week, new students were encouraged to join various societies, athletic organisations and meet new friends. (Leicester Mercury Media Group, courtesy of Leicester University Archives)

new Ashley Clarke science block and to the other, the Percy Gee Students' Union building with its offices, catering and entertainment facilities that was opened by the Queen in 1958. Opposite the Percy Gee was College Hall, the women's hall of residence where I had stayed during my January visit. As befitted Leicester's recently-acquired independent university status, a major building programme was under way, including a new chemistry block and the replacement of College Hall by a new women's residence in Knighton, a nearby suburb of Leicester. By the end of my time at the university many other structures had been erected including the innovative and award-winning Engineering Tower designed by James Stirling that was opened in 1963.

At registration I confirmed my choice of Pure Mathematics as my three year main subject and chose Applied Mathematics and Logic and Scientific Method as subsidiary subjects, the latter a last minute substitute for the Physics that I so dreaded. After registration I made my way to the Percy Gee building where I joined a massive queue waiting for refreshments in the downstairs coffee bar. As luck would have it, I discovered that the group of six or more first year students next to me in the queue were also taking the Pure Mathematics course. Organising the group like a mother hen was Jean, a strikingly handsome rather than decoratively pretty, young woman from Bournemouth, who had the admirable knack of making insecure first year males feel

The lunch queue in the Percy Gee. Queues were a common feature of student life in the early 1960s. (Leicester Mercury Media Group, courtesy of Leicester University Archives)

special and at ease. It was no coincidence that her entourage consisted mainly of hopeful young men vying for her attention from that day forward.

I could hardly believe my luck when, later in the week, Jean said that she had been invited to a Geography Society party and asked if I would like to go with her. Naturally I said yes and with barely contained excitement arrived at the appointed time and place to meet only to find that she was also accompanied by a diminutive and extremely shy female companion. At the party, the three of us were greeted enthusiastically by a second year geography student and it soon became apparent to me that he was the reason for Jean's invitation and that I was there to partner her friend. My disappointment was tempered somewhat when, as the alcohol began to flow, my designated companion for the evening became considerably less shy and proved to be a very good dancer.

To celebrate the end of Freshers' Week and the return of the second and third year students, a large Saturday dance was held in the main Queen's Hall at the Percy Gee, appropriately named the Integration Hop. As an inexperienced first year student, I unpacked my best suit, polished my shoes and proceeded excitedly to the dance anticipating meeting some new friends, hopefully from the opposite sex. However, this was an occasion where the predatory males among the rest of the student body took the opportunity to survey the incoming female talent in the first year intake. Inexperienced first year males, like myself, had little chance with the better-looking female newcomers because the recently returned older and more confident second and third year students soon homed in on their prey, especially the loud and normally inebriated members of the university's Rugby Club. Jean was there, still accompanied by her geographer. Despite some vain efforts on my part, her geographer persisted and within a year they were engaged. My one opportunity, an unexpected close encounter during our third year on the back row seats of the Wednesday night Film Club, failed as she was far too well chaperoned by her female associates.

'For the women, the first obstacle has already been encountered – the Integration Hop. To return home unaccompanied from this is to fall, or at any rate stumble, at the first fence; but, not to worry, there are other hops – and console yourself with the thought that some don't even start the course.'

Janus, *Ripple*, 24 October 1960

The return of the second year students gave an immediate impetus to the social life in Southmeade. Their knowledge of the university and the night life of the city proved invaluable because like all the other first year students I was desperately trying to find

A break for drinks during the Integration Hop. (Leicester Mercury Media Group, courtesy of Leicester University Archives)

my way around a new and unfamiliar environment. The room that I shared with Roger and David was once the original lounge of Southmeade House, the largest in the building and, unfortunately for us, it had come to be used as an unofficial common room by the rest of the resident students. Card games, chess competitions and serious and intense discussions regularly continued well into the early hours of the morning, frequently depriving Roger, David and me of the opportunity to study and to sleep.

All too often, our discussions focused on women and sex, a topic with which we seemed to be obsessed. Out of the seven first year students at Southmeade, only one admitted that he had had full sexual intercourse, an admission that he subsequently regretted because he was forced to describe the process with full and explicit details on numerous occasions. Whether or not we were typical young men of those days, it was clear that our knowledge of sex was mostly theoretical. At school, we had all been taught the mechanics of human reproduction, what went where and why, but we were all ignorant of the finer details regarding the emotions, sensations and techniques associated with the act. At home, sex was never discussed. Mother considered any mention of it to be 'dirty talk'. It was not surprising that, until my days at Southmeade, I had discovered more about sexual techniques from the graffiti drawn on the cubical walls in the toilets of Norwich's Surrey Street Bus Station than from any formal tuition. So it was in the true spirit of scientific enquiry that my inexperienced friends and I continually interrogated our experienced colleague, in the hope that we would be properly prepared when our opportunity finally arrived.

My childhood had ended many years before with the discovery of girls, or rather the discovery that girls were mysteriously attractive, that having a special girlfriend was exciting and enhanced my standing among my contemporaries, and that kissing was a great pleasure. My first proper girlfriend materialised when I was just 15, a chance liaison that occurred as a result of a Mighty Atom firework, carefully placed and detonated by my friend Tony at the 5 November village bonfire party, which had thrown a screaming 15-year-old female into my arms and where she stayed for the rest of the display. For a few weeks thereafter we met on the veranda of 'the hut', a small green wooden building on the village Playing Field that was used as a changing room by the cricket and football teams. Sadly, our relationship did not endure as, in time, my innocence became all too clear and she moved on to a more experienced companion. I had held hands in primary school, enjoyed postman's knock at parties and endured the fantasies and crushes of my early teens, but my inexperience was betrayed because my conversation was limited, my fumbling aimless and my kissing technique suspect.

Before my bonfire adventure I had fantasised in teenage fashion over several local young women, but despite spending many hours cycling past their homes or trying to gain their attention when joining the gangs of young people that frequently collected on the Playing Field, I had been unsuccessful in love. At 14 years of age my greatest teenage crush was for Linda, a mature 15-year-old from a farmstead adjacent to my home. Every morning, Linda and I travelled on the service bus to school in Great Yarmouth and every morning I contrived to sit by her. Throughout the half-hour journey, Linda talked and I listened attentively. My hopes came to nothing as Linda had a 19-year-old boyfriend and she clearly did not consider a pimply 14-year-old to be a suitable contender for her affections. My resolve to wait for an opportune moment was also dashed when, in 1956, Linda and her family moved away to Great Yarmouth and we lost contact. For many years afterwards, I was able to follow Linda's progress with interest and unfulfilled passion because she became a leading actress and singer in the Great Yarmouth Operatic and Dramatic Society, and had starring roles in many of their Christmas pantomimes, but we never crossed paths again. Linda eventually became a professional singer and had a minor hit record in 1964 with *Love is a Many Splendored Thing* under her professional stage name of Linda Saxone.

At 16, I was allowed by my parents to attend dances in neighbouring village halls and to visit the cinema unaccompanied. Before then I normally went to dances and film shows with my parents, and rarely on my own. In a more restrictive age, my freedom was limited and I was expected to return home by 10pm with an extension to 11pm on special occasions. According to my parents, anyone out later than 11.00 at night was definitely up to no good. Nevertheless, dances and film shows provided me with many opportunities to find girlfriends, usually a chance meeting in a dance hall which was consolidated by an invitation to the cinema and a seat in the back-row of the stalls. Not that I was in any way a great Casanova as, on more occasions than not, I returned home from a dance having failed to find a kissing partner, my advances having been rebuffed or worse, ignored. This mattered little to me as I enjoyed dancing and the social atmosphere at a village hall gathering. I was 17 before I had my first long-term relationship, one where possible plans for the future were discussed and a kiss at the end of the evening was not the only objective. Yet, despite my many endeavours in that respect, like many of my new student friends I arrived at university still unaccomplished in the practice of sex.

One of the joys of university life was the frequent and often lively discussions that were held in our room at Southmeade, in the Percy Gee Junior Common Room (better known as the JCR), the coffee bar and, more formally, at the regular Friday night meetings of the Debating Society in the Queen's Hall, discussions where we argued and considered all kinds of intellectual, moral and political issues. Discussions in which all shades of opinion were expressed relating to contemporary issues such as capital punishment, nuclear disarmament, homosexuality, racial discrimination, advertising, religion and politics. Not that I held many strong opinions or beliefs on any issue and I could often see virtues at the same time in opposing points of view. I had been brought up by my parents to defer to the views of my 'elders and betters' and I frequently adhered to their beliefs without question. At Great Yarmouth Grammar School I held the masters in awe, with their confident manner and academic gowns, and never questioned their strictures or considered their views to be anything other than the truth. I certainly never had the confidence to challenge any of their convictions. It was a personal revelation to find myself among lively and open minds that explored issues in detail before making judgements and to discover that my thoughts and opinions were considered to be worthy of consideration.

Late night sessions in Southmeade frequently ended in loud and raucous horseplay, an inevitable feature of an all-male society. On one occasion, when I was the yelling victim pinned down under a pile of laughing students, the hilarity was ended by the arrival of the postgraduate resident from upstairs who threatened to report our poor behaviour to the warden. To my embarrassment, I found myself apologising to him for having used bad language. At home in Norfolk swearing was taboo. As far as I can recollect, nobody in my working-class family either swore or used blasphemies as part of their normal speech. In fact, swearing in general seemed to be less common than it is today, or at least it was then in my Norfolk home at Rollesby. For most of us, the f-word was not part of our everyday language. According to my mother, any man who swore was beneath contempt and if a woman swore, she was 'as common as muck'. Swearing was bad manners and manners were important. For my parents, success was achieved through education and good manners, a lesson that was instilled in me throughout the whole of my childhood. 'Manners maketh man' and 'a gentleman is defined by his manners' were frequently repeated sayings and I was trained by my mother to give up my seat on the bus, to open doors for a lady, to tip my cap to my betters, to know how to behave at the table, not to talk while I was eating, to watch my Ps and Qs and all the other attributes and behaviours that she considered to be essential for respectability. I now find that the lessons I learned then are difficult to undo in these modern times of equality and political correctness, even if I wished to do so.

My first social engagement at university was when I received a formal invitation to a drinks party in the main Beaumont Hall complex organised by one of the newly

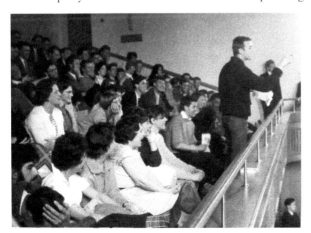

returned second year students. When I arrived I was greeted by my host who, to my great surprise, was dressed formally in a

Debates were often riotous affairs and speakers were regularly heckled, especially by the noisy and rebellious students on the balcony.

black suit, polished shoes, white shirt and black bow tie. Most of his other guests were similarly attired. Dressed in my cavalry twill trousers, green shirt, tie and sports jacket, I felt somewhat out of place. Drinks consisted mainly of dry sherry which was consumed in some quantity by the other all male party goers. I satisfied myself with a fruit juice. At home, sherry, together with port, was a Christmas drink and a tipple mainly for women and the older generation. Even then it was usually sweet sherry, not the dry sherry served by my student friends, a variety that I soon discovered wreaked havoc with my stomach.

CHAPTER 3

A CAMPUS IN CONFLICT

Once lectures began, weekdays at Leicester became a routine. I rose at 7.30am in time for a quick wash before breakfast at Beaumont Hall, and then on to the university by cycle. At least, that was the theory. After a late night discussion or an evening on the town, the wash and breakfast were often missed in a futile attempt not to be late for the first teaching session of the morning. Most of my day was spent in the Percy Gee with occasional visits to the Fielding Johnson for lectures, tutorials and the library. The Percy Gee building was the home of the Leicester University Students' Union and the centre for the university's social life. The building itself, which was built into the side of a hill, consisted of a maze of corridors, stairways and rooms on three or more levels.

The main entrance of the Percy Gee was approached up a set of semi-circular stairs and opened out into a rectangular reception hall. A passage immediately to the right led down to various union offices, and a stairway to the left led to the male and female cloakrooms, pigeon holes for letters and other communications, a squash court and a room used for table tennis. Further along and to the right of the reception hall was the

The Percy Gee Building, opened by the Queen in 1958, was home to the Leicester University Students' Union. I spent most of my free time socialising in the Percy Gee. (Leicester Mercury Media Group)

Everything happened in the Queen's Hall; debates, dances, film shows, concerts, theatrical performances and, sometimes, a first date. (Leicester Mercury Media Group)

Queen's Hall, a large wood-panelled function room equipped with a stage area and a balcony, which was used as the venue for dances, film shows, dramatic productions and the monthly Friday night debates. At the far end of the reception hall was the JCR, a place to sit and talk between lectures, and which, at times, was used as the location for long and often costly games of poker and bridge. An open spiral staircase led down to a long wide corridor off which the coffee bar, the university bookshop and the dining hall were located. The same staircase also led to rooms on the upper floor, one of which was eventually used as a television room and where I spent many hours in the summer watching test match cricket.

Lectures for the General Science degree were located in the Fielding Johnson Building and held in classrooms reminiscent of my school days that were simply furnished with a blackboard, desks and chairs. The standard of lectures was variable. The Pure Mathematics course was delivered by a postgraduate who was working his way to a doctorate and clearly had little interest in either teaching or the difficulties of his students. Fortunately, the material was familiar, thanks to the extra mathematics classes in my third year in the grammar school's sixth form. I was also directed to a textbook in the university bookshop which covered the subject matter of the lectures almost word for word. The Applied Mathematics course was little better. Attendance at lectures was a compulsory requirement and we were all expected to sign our names on a register. But Jean came to the rescue and took responsibility for her circle of young men, signing for us whenever we were absent. She also made excellent notes which we regularly borrowed and copied. The Logic and Scientific Method course was different. This was an extremely interesting course organised by a charismatic New Zealander, Rom Harré, who was clearly destined for great things. His course explored the nature and structure of argument and proof, especially as applied in science.

In 1959, the university was still only two years old as an independent institution and, as a consequence, had yet to develop a recognisable 'Leicester' style. There was some originality in the courses offered, but the character of both the university and its Students' Union was still evolving. As the majority of its staff and students were drawn from the conservative middle classes it was not surprising that there was an initial attempt to emulate the traditions of Oxford and Cambridge. It soon became apparent that there was an extremely vocal and active minority, mostly drawn from the growing number of working-class students at the university, who were agitating for a change from the traditional Oxbridge format towards a more liberal campus, with less authority and greater individual freedoms.

The university's main administration block was named the Fielding Johnson Building in honour of the Leicester clothing manufacturer who bought it in 1921 to house the proposed University College of Leicester.

Many students wore their gowns with pride, some even donned blazers with the university's coat of arms on the breast pocket. Beaumont Hall students, 1959. (R. Davies)

The wearing of gowns became the pivotal issue. A proposal had been tabled by the university's governing body, the Senate, that students should be compelled to wear gowns at lectures, tutorials and other official functions – a move resisted by many in the Students' Union. Prior to starting my course I had purchased an undergraduate gown by post from the firm of Ede and Ravenscroft for the princely sum of £4 5s 6d. Once I had overcome my initial embarrassment, I wore my gown with pride because it represented a hard-won achievement on my part. I enjoyed being special and the thought that I was among the first from my Norfolk family to achieve this distinction. Yet there were many students who objected to compulsion and successfully rebelled against the proposal. Their voice was ultimately dominant and most lectures became gown-free, so my gown was consigned to decay in my trunk. Although I publicly celebrated a victory over authoritarianism, along with many of my student companions, privately I felt cheated. For some, this issue was seen as part of the developing conflict between the staff and students from the traditional conservative right, those who held the positions of power within the university and the Students' Union at the time, on the one hand and the proponents of working-class socialism on the other; although many of the most vociferous exponents of theoretical socialism were themselves from the middle classes. It was a conflict that was starting to take place in many universities and not just Leicester.

Academic dress

What is it about our gowns that makes so many in our fraternity want to tear them off. Why is it that even before the proud occupant is out of lecture his 85s academic dress is firmly, deftly and self-consciously stuffed into a delightful attaché case. Does the gown represent the sure sign of the naïve little fresher and to be treated with deference and superiority? Or are we to believe the oft-quoted protest that it is a crude and blatant copying of the two elder (and most beloved) Universities. The situation becomes awkwardly apparent where there are some in our midst who look impressively scholarly and others anything but. When some wear their gown as proof of achievements past and others use them as an admirable pen wiper, present.

Letters, *Ripple*, 6 November 1959

Within Leicester's Students' Union, the splits were slowly becoming apparent, even as early as 1960. The President of the Union, an articulate young man who was at home in a suit, represented the side of tradition. He had the confidence and know-how for public speaking, and was a suitable figurehead for entertaining distinguished guests of the Union, especially at the controversial reception and dinner held immediately before the annual Union Ball. It was controversial not only because formal dress was a requirement, dinner jackets for the men and evening gowns for the women, but also because many students could barely afford a ticket to attend. Tickets to the ball alone cost 7s 6d each and were affordable to most students, but the tickets that also included the preceding sherry reception and dinner cost £1 10s 0d each and were far too expensive for many, including me. Additionally, a dinner jacket was not part of my wardrobe and hire costs were too prohibitive.

In an attempt to demonstrate the progressive nature of the Students' Union, much was made of the fact that the student body had, for the first time, elected a woman to be vice-president. Despite working hard in her post, which potentially advanced the case for women in official positions, she was still regarded by many of her student contemporaries as being simply a lively but decorative consort for the president. Most of the officers that made up the controlling body of the Union, the Students' Representative Council (SRC), were male traditionalists and fought hard to develop Leicester University along Oxbridge lines. The issue of gowns

Dinner jackets were expensive to hire.

Another West End Clothiers Service

Hire Dept.

BE CORRECTLY DRESSED FOR ALL OCCASIONS

Well Dressed Gentlemen avail themselves of this excellent Hire Service offered by

THE WEST END CLOTHIERS LTD.
BLACKBIRD ROAD, LEICESTER
Telephone: 22533/4

CHARGES FOR HIRE

Morning Dress		*Evening Dress*	
Morning Suit . . .	45/-	Evening Dress Suit . .	45/-
Morning Suit and Hat .	52/6	Evening Dress Coat . .	30/-
Morning Coat . . .	30/-	Evening Dress Vest . .	10/6
Waistcoat, Grey or Black .	10/6	Evening Dress Trousers .	10/6
Trousers, striped . .	10/6	D.B. Dinner Suit. From 25/- to 45/-	
Black Lounge Jacket (D.B. or S.B.) and Striped		S.B. Dinner Suit, Shawl Collar, From 25/- to 45/- (with black or maroon	
Trousers . . .	37/6	Cummerbund)	
Black Lounge Jacket .	25/-	D.B. Dinner Jacket . .	37/6
Overcoat . . .	30/-	S.B. Dinner Jacket Shawl Collar . .	37/6
Grey or Black Top Hat .	10/6	S.B. Dinner Suit . .	32/6
Shirt and Collar . .	9/-	S.B. Dinner Jacket & Vest	25/6
Grey or Black Tie . .	2/6	Shirt and Collar . .	9/-
Grey or Chamois Gloves .	4/6	Bow: Black, Maroon, White	2/6
Shoes	7/6	Patent Shoes . . .	7/6

HIRE WITH COMPLETE CONFIDENCE

Leicester city centre and memorial clock tower. The city was an exciting place for a country-born Norfolk boy.

had become the test case. The SRC passed a motion to support the Senate's proposal for wearing them, but the motion failed to gain the approval of the whole student body and was subsequently overturned at a general meeting of the Students' Union.

The characters of the Union, those of a more unconventional and liberal turn of mind, were mainly associated with the Entertainments and RAG committees. They were a set of charismatic young people who attracted me not just because they were different, exciting and prepared to challenge accepted principles, but also because they had fun. This group of confident, jazz-loving men and women became my role models at university, the type of student that I aspired to become.

Leicester in the late 1950s was a bustling prosperous Midlands industrial city whose wealth was based on light engineering and the production of hosiery, textiles and footwear. The population of about 300,000 was predominantly white working class, together with small but rapidly growing communities of Irish, Eastern European, African-Caribbean and Asian descent. At the heart of Leicester stood a 70ft high Gothic style Clock Tower, erected in 1868 as a memorial to four of the city's past benefactors, and around which was located the main shopping area, a wholesale fruit, vegetable and fish market and most of Leicester's entertainment facilities. My first trip into the city centre was to buy a university scarf from Knights Outfitters in Granby Street. The claret, white and green striped scarf was an essential article of clothing for most first year students and one which emphatically declared 'Look at me, I am a university student', one of the elite five per cent.

My first shopping expedition was to Knight's on Granby Street where I bought the university scarf that emphatically declared 'Look at me, I am a university student.'

My first serious relationship at Leicester was with Joanna, whom I met while dancing in the university's Cellar Jazz Club. She was a tall and extremely good looking final year student of fashion and design from the Leicester College of Art and Technology (the Art and Tech), who was blessed with an excellent model figure. Joanna was so impressively tall that she frequently wore flat shoes in an attempt not to tower over me. I delighted in her company and revelled in the envious looks of my fellow male students. Joanna was classy, always elegant, and expensively and beautifully dressed. What she saw in me I cannot tell, as I was frequently described by my close companions as a badly wrapped parcel, even when dressed in my best clothes.

Joanna was definitely middle class and her parents were professional people. In rural Norfolk I could never have aspired to an association with a young woman from her background. When I told my parents about Joanna, my mother's response was to warn me against becoming involved with 'blue stockings', fortune hunters and women I could not afford. Her advice was that I should find myself a nice factory girl who would look after me properly and bear my children. Yet, university society provided a level playing field, albeit a temporary one, and the opportunity to associate with young people from all social backgrounds. To potential new friends we were all simply students and, in that respect, equal and classless. Not that my background mattered at all to Joanna and we spent much of the autumn and early spring terms of 1959 and

1960 enjoying each other's company at dances, the Cellar Jazz Club, in private tête-à-têtes at various coffee bars and public houses in Leicester, and at the Christmas Ball where we danced until 3am to music from the Danny Rogers Orchestra.

Nevertheless, to some female students backgrounds did matter because for many middle and working-class families, further education for women was seen as an unnecessary luxury and university simply as an opportunity to make an advantageous marriage rather than the foundation of a successful long-term career. Many female friends from my teenage years in Norfolk envisaged nothing beyond school other than temporary employment before marriage and motherhood. Some intelligent young women even chose to marry rather than attend a college or a university, a choice that they may have regretted in later life. At Leicester, one nubile first year student gained great notoriety as she moved from one potentially eligible bachelor to another in a barely-disguised attempt to find a suitable catch – a quest that included myself, albeit briefly. She eventually disappeared from her course amid rumours of an impending marriage to a well-to-do third year student.

Joanna, on the other hand, was far too sensible and understood full well that this was not the time for a permanent relationship. I was in the first year of a three year course and she was about to take her final examinations before embarking on her chosen career designing fashionable clothes, a strategy that required her full attention in the medium term and would most probably involve a move to London. She had things to do and goals to achieve, a process that she outlined to me at length. At the time, I found it difficult to understand that a young woman could put a career before personal relationships and possible marriage, even if only temporarily. Not to be outdone, in 'Walter Mitty' fashion, I invented some goals of my own – a first-class degree, a trip to America, a doctorate at Yale and many other totally impossible dreams. Reluctantly, we decided to remain simply as friends for the moment. But when we did occasionally meet, by accident or design, the time was never right to be anything other than friends.

Life in hall took a surprising turn one evening during the spring term when Southmeade was visited by three nurses. This was an unexpected treat for us because young women were rarely seen in a men's hall of residence in those days. At the time of their arrival most of Southmeade's residents were engaged in a card game with Roger, David and me in our ground floor accommodation. Our visitors explained that they were conducting an official inspection of all the university's halls of residence in an attempt to improve hygiene and requested permission to visit our rooms. Naturally there were no objections, so we continued our card game while the nurses made their inspection. Eventually, they returned, expressed their thanks and left.

The real reason for the visit became obvious at bedtime when we discovered that most of our pyjama trousers and dressing gowns had lost their cords, no doubt carried off in triumph as trophies to one of Leicester's nurses' homes. A council of war decided that our invaders most probably came from the Royal Infirmary nurses' training hostel that was located in Brookfield, a large Victorian house not too far away on the London Road. Although it was nearly midnight, we decided to make an immediate retaliatory visit in an attempt to retrieve our lost pyjama cords. Exactly how we would get them back was not at all clear but, undaunted, 10 or more excited male students cycled from Southmeade and arrived on the lawn in front of the large half-timbered black-and-white house where we thought that they might be located.

Although the house was in darkness, an open window close to an outside balcony on the upper floor enabled one of our more nimble colleagues to gain access to the inside of the hostel. After a while, the main door to the building opened and our house-breaking adventurer appeared, accompanied by two young women dressed in their nightclothes. Luckily, the open window had led into a student nurse's bedroom and not into the room of the resident tutor in charge. Eventually, we were joined on the lawn by most of the other student nurses, who greatly enjoyed the joke but confessed in hushed voices that our pyjama cord raiders did not come from their house. To compensate for being disturbed in the early hours of the morning, we arranged to meet our new friends the following evening at a local hostelry, a meeting that resulted in the formation of some new and close relationships. Flushed with this success, during the next two weeks we raided all the women's halls of residence within two miles of Southmeade, but our pyjama cords were never recovered.

CHAPTER 4

A ROCK 'N' ROLL REVOLUTION

In rural Rollesby, Richard was the first of my teenage friends to own a modern electric record player; a red and cream Dansette with an automatic record changing mechanism that could play both the old 78rpm shellac records and the newer unbreakable vinyl 45rpm singles and EPs, and 33rpm LPs. My Miller grandparents owned an old wind-up gramophone on which they played their collection of 78rpm 1930s dance band music, but this was consigned to the garage when the wind-up mechanism broke down. I spent many hours with Richard in the kitchen at his home listening to his record collection, which consisted mainly of dance band music and songs by Bing Crosby, Doris Day, Ruby Murray and Frank Sinatra. We sang along with Bing Crosby to his rendition of *White Christmas* and hummed to the strains of *The Westminster Waltz* and *The Coronation Scott*. Our lives changed in the autumn of 1956 when Richard bought a copy of an LP entitled *Elvis Presley; Rock 'n' roll Volume 1*. We had heard of the new sensational American music called rock 'n' roll and had even listened to some rock 'n' roll recordings played on the radio, but this was the first real experience of this musical genre for us both. Straight away we were hooked as we sang along to *Blue Suede Shoes*, *Heartbreak Hotel*, *That's all right Momma*, *Money Honey* and *Lawdy Miss Clawdy*. From that moment on Crosby, Day, Murray and Sinatra were considered 'old hat'.

My newly discovered enthusiasm for rock 'n' roll was consolidated in that November when the film *Rock Around the Clock* was shown at the Regal Cinema in Great Yarmouth. Excited by reports of rioting, seat slashing by Teddy Boys and unruly behaviour during performances of the film in London, Manchester and many other major cities throughout the country, I joined the long queue of young people outside the Regal Cinema, not sure what to expect. Despite the best efforts of the usherettes and the cinema management to control the teenage audience, I was not disappointed because screams and shouts greeted the appearance of the various rock 'n' roll stars on the screen and many couples attempted to dance to the music on the stairs and in the gangways. Although the story-line was weak, the music of Bill Haley and his Comets, Freddie Bell and his Bellboys, and the Platters was greatly appreciated. One rock 'n' roll standard followed another, including *Rock around the Clock*, *See you later Alligator*, *Razzle Dazzle* and *R-O-C-K Rock* from Bill Haley, and *Only You* and *The Great Pretender* from the Platters.

When I was 15, I was struck down by a lengthy bout of gastric 'flu and confined to bed for a number of days. In one of his rare but genuine demonstrations of affection and concern, my father bought a second-hand wireless for my bedroom, a large brown and cream valve radio with six push buttons for pre-selected stations. After that, I spent much of my time alone in my bedroom working at my homework or staring out of the bedroom window listening to programmes of my choice. It was clearly purchased by my father in self-defence because, in true teenage style, I had begun to argue with my parents about our choice of radio programmes. Inevitably, my tastes were starting to differ from theirs. Other than various comedy shows, the quiz game *Top of the Form*, *Journey into Space*, *The Goon Show* and, from 1957, *The Saturday Skiffle Club*, I followed the fashion of the time by listening mainly to Radio Luxembourg.

Radio Luxembourg was an American style English language commercial radio station transmitted from the Grand Duchy of Luxembourg every evening from 7pm on 208 metres in the Medium wave, a station that was normally introduced as 'Your Station of the Stars'. Its programmes were a mixture of music and variety, interspersed with commercial advertising. Throughout the evening, I was encouraged to drink Horlicks and Ovaltine, and to use Horace Batchelor's method for winning the football pools. At first I paid more attention to the variety shows, following the adventures of Dan Dare, Pilot of the Future (based on the character from the *Eagle* comic), marvelling at the sporting knowledge of Leslie Welsh the 'Memory Man' and listening intently to the contestants competing on Hughie Green's *Opportunity Knocks*. I shouted answers at the radio during editions of *Take Your Pick* and *Double Your Money*, on Irish night I sang 'If you're Irish come into the Parlour' and I memorised and sung along with many of the commercial jingles. But, by the age of 16, it was the music that attracted me to Radio Luxembourg; big band music from the likes of Edmundo Ross and Billy May, songs from contemporary singing stars and crooners, and the latest rock 'n' roll recordings, many of which were banned by the BBC.

Most record companies sponsored shows on Radio Luxembourg that featured their latest releases, including Phillips' *Record Rendezvous*, *The Capitol Show* introduced by Mike Thompson, and Benny Lee's *Record Hop* which publicised recordings from Columbia and Parlophone. But the most popular programmes for followers of rock 'n' roll were Guss Gordon's Saturday night *Jamboree*, which included a 30 minute spot in which Alan Freed introduced the latest rock 'n' roll releases from America, and the 11pm Sunday night *British Top 20* introduced initially by Keith Fordyce who was subsequently replaced by Barry Alldis in 1958. Many Sunday evenings were spent with my ear pressed hard against the speaker of my radio with its volume turned down low trying to catch the latest pop music news without disturbing my sleeping parents in their bedroom next door.

Like many of my friends, by the end of 1956 I was a rock 'n' roll enthusiast. It was exciting music, it was music with a beat, it was music for dancing and it was the music of the young. Rock 'n' roll music – a fusion of Black American Rhythm and Blues with White Country and Western music – developed in the USA during the early 1950s. It was a musical style that was performed by young people for young people, and conventionally played on amplified electric guitars with a heavy accentuated beat designed to induce foot-tapping and an inclination to dance in a relatively wild and abandoned manner. The fact that many grown-ups disliked rock 'n' roll and the trappings and fashions associated with it, gave it added spice – even more so when we realised that rock 'n' roll was slang for sexual intercourse among black Americans, a fact that few adults appreciated! So it was most disconcerting when my mother announced that she had heard a very nice rock 'n' roll song on the radio – *Singing the Blues* by Tommy Steele. Mothers were not supposed to like rock 'n' roll. After that, I viewed Tommy Steele with great suspicion, although I liked the record too.

Television reception improved immensely throughout Norfolk when the Tacolneston transmitter became operational in the spring of 1957. So, like many other Norfolk residents, my father bought our first television, a Bush 14 inch black and white set that quickly took pride of place in our small living room, relegating the radio to the sideboard. The black and white pictures were often unclear because the reception was variable and susceptible to interference from poor atmospheric conditions, passing traffic and electronic machinery, particularly the milking machines at the farm opposite to our house. Until 1959, when Anglia Television came on line, it was only possible to receive broadcasts from the one BBC station and, consequently, there was no choice of programmes. Nevertheless, my parents were hooked and watching television became their main form of entertainment in the evenings. For them, trips to the dance hall and the cinema became a thing of the past, despite the newly arrived attractions of films in glorious Technicolor, cinemascope and wrap round sound, there was even a brief experiment with 3D vision. Once television arrived, the dance hall and the cinema were abandoned by many of the older generation leaving them to become primarily the domain of the young.

Once the initial novelty had worn off, my interest in television waned. I much preferred to play sport, dance, visit the cinema, hang out with my friends and chase girls. Nevertheless, some programmes held my interest – mainly those covering sporting activities, quizzes and popular music. I even developed an interest in golf and

Skiffle groups became popular through the *Six-Five Special*.

rugby through television, games unfamiliar and unaffordable to most working-class youngsters. But my favourite programme of all was the Saturday night edition of the *Six-Five Special*, a magazine programme for young people that included a major element of popular beat music, mainly rock 'n' roll, skiffle and jazz, as well as comedy sketches, interviews and educational items. It was an innovative live show with an invited audience of trendy young people that was broadcast by the BBC from February 1957 until December 1958. Introduced by Pete Murray, Josephine Douglas and the boxer, Freddy Mills, the weekly shows included comedy from Spike Milligan and Bernie Winters, guitar instruction from Bert Weedon, information about youth activities and interviews with popular celebrities, in-between live performances of popular music.

Every Saturday without fail I watched many of my favourite rock 'n' roll artists sing their latest hit records, including Tommy Steele, Terry Dene, Craig Douglas, Russ Hamilton, Jim Dale, the King Brothers and Marty Wilde, occasionally backed by the resident bands, Don Lang and his Frantic Five or the John Barry Seven. I heard skiffle from Lonnie Donegan, Chas McDevitt, Nancy Whiskey, the Eden Street Skiffle Band, The Vipers and Bob Cort's Skiffle Group, and jazz from Johnnie Dankworth, Cleo Lane, and Chris Barber and his Band. I even tolerated Michael Holliday's crooning and the sickly niceness of Petula Clark. Through watching the *Six-Five Special* I became aware of the current fashionable trends in clothing and hairstyles, the technicalities of rock 'n' roll dancing and the specialised language of the young. People were classified as 'hep cats', 'cool dudes', 'ace chicks' or 'squares', I danced at a 'hop' where the 'joint' was often 'jumping', and I said 'See you later alligator' instead of 'Goodbye' to which the expected reply was 'In a while, crocodile'.

By 1957, I considered rock 'n' roll to be not just a musical genre but, first and foremost, music for dancing rock 'n' roll style – a new dance for the young, an exciting and energetic dance derived from jitterbug and jive. Any music that provided the rhythmic beat for this fast, bouncy and spinning dance was rock 'n' roll music to me. In my mind, skiffle was simply a variation of rock 'n' roll music, because I found that it was just as easy to dance in a rock 'n' roll style to Lonnie Donegan's version of *The Ballad of New Orleans* as it was to Bill Haley's *Rock around the Clock*. And so, skiffle, as popularised by many British bands, but especially by Lonnie Donegan and his Skiffle

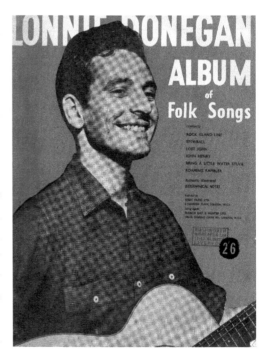

I danced to Donegan's music.

Group, I regarded as the British version of rock 'n' roll music. The advantage of skiffle over imported rock 'n' roll was that it was relatively simple to play with acoustic guitars and home-made percussion instruments (washboards and tea-chest basses), and did not depend upon the expensive electrical amplification that was used by most American rock 'n' roll bands. Consequently, ordinary British youngsters could afford to play in a skiffle band and many teenagers danced rock 'n' roll to their music. In 1958, even I played in a village skiffle band.

Dancing was a passion with me. From the age of 15, I had attended a local dance on most weekends, usually at the community halls in various Norfolk villages. At first I went with my family, but eventually I toured the local dance halls with groups of my teenage friends after my parents had become addicted to television. My mother and father were very good dancers and had taught me the moves for most ballroom dances. I knew the basic steps for the waltz, the foxtrot and quickstep, as well as the veleta, the Gay Gordons and the St Bernard's Waltz. As a result, I had little difficulty in finding dance partners although the best looking females were always in great demand and often unattainable. Music for dancing was usually provided by live bands made up from village musicians who performed unaided by microphones or amplification equipment. When a live band was unavailable, music was provided by records played on a radiogram.

Although I had seen rock 'n' roll dancing at the cinema and on television, for a while I had little opportunity to learn the dance. Many dance halls had discouraged rock 'n' roll dancing as it was considered to be unsociable and a potential hazard for older dancers. Nevertheless, my first experience of rock 'n' roll dancing was a demonstration during the interval at a village Saturday dance. I watched the twirling couple with amazement, excited by the dance they were demonstrating and the brief glimpses of stocking top, knickers and suspender. When the demonstration was over we were all given an introductory lesson as part of the evening's entertainment. My tuition was completed at the Eels Foot Inn, a Broad-side public house a mile from my Rollesby home. The Eels Foot was a popular summer waterside evening stopover for coach tours from Great Yarmouth and the Caister and Hemsby Holiday Camps, and entertainment was provided in an old wooden boathouse which had been converted into a dance hall. At weekends, music was played by a live band but on weekdays music was provided by records played on a radiogram. To cater for the large number of local young people who regularly visited the Eels Foot dance hall, most of the records played were current rock 'n' roll recordings and rock 'n' roll dancing was permitted. Along with many local teenagers, I was a regular early evening visitor to the Eels Foot Inn

The Eels Foot Inn, the waterside public house in Norfolk where I learnt to rock 'n' roll.

during the summer months of 1957, where I sang along to my favourite songs, *Diana* by Paul Anka, *Last Train to San Fernando* from Johnny Duncan and Elvis' *All Shook Up*, while improving my rock 'n' roll dancing skills at a time when I should have been doing my school homework.

By the time I was 18, I had joined with many of my sixth form colleagues to dance at the larger ballrooms in Great Yarmouth and Gorleston to music played by their professional orchestras. My regular venues were the Floral Hall in Gorleston, with Bert Galey's Orchestra, and the New Gari Ballroom in Great Yarmouth, with the Gordon Edwards Sextet and Rollesby's ex-resident and my former neighbour, Linda, as the female vocalist. Initially rock 'n' roll dancing was discouraged in both of these ballrooms, while in some of Great Yarmouth's other dance halls it was banned altogether. However, like cinema audiences, attendance at public dances declined when television established itself as an alternative attraction. As dance halls became primarily the province of the young, it was natural that dances would cater more for their tastes and that rock 'n' roll and jiving would become tolerated, usually as an alternative to the quickstep.

Rock 'n' roll was not the only new dance adopted by younger dancers. In 1958, the craze was for the cha-cha, a derivative of the Latin-American mambo that had been a popular dance during the mid-1950s. The cha-cha was promoted by the Ted Heath Band, Tommy Dorsey and Eddie Calvert through instrumental hit records such as *Tea for Two Cha-Cha*, *Cha-Cha in the Rain*, *Trumpet Cha-Cha* and *Never on a Sunday*. In 1958, I joined the long lines of under 30s dancing the cha-cha in unison across the dance floor at the Floral Hall. By 1959, skiffle, with its origins in jazz, led many young people to discover traditional jazz music. Lonnie Donegan was himself first and foremost a jazz musician and playing skiffle was his party piece during intervals at jazz concerts. Not that jazz music was new to British youngsters. In the early 1950s, traditional New Orleans jazz had undergone a revival in Britain through the efforts of jazz musicians like Great Yarmouth born Ken Colyer, Chris Barber, Humphrey Littleton, George Melly and Johnny Dankworth. Through BBC television's *Six-Five Special*, as well as the specialist jazz programmes broadcast on Radio Luxembourg and the BBC Light Programme (including Saturday night's *Jazz Club* on the BBC), jazz reached a wider audience and became popular with young people, particularly with students, and also with me because jazz music also provided the ideal rhythm for rock 'n' roll dancing. I joined many of my sixth form friends to dance rock 'n' roll at various Norfolk jazz clubs, upsetting many of the older jazz aficionados and bearded sweater-wearing beatniks who preferred to sit and listen to the music rather than dance. The wider popularity of jazz became evident when Chris Barber's recording of Sidney Bechet's *Petite Fleur* entered the rock 'n' roll dominated hit parade in February 1959, followed soon after by Acker Bilk's *Summer Set*. Rock 'n' roll, skiffle and jazz were known collectively as 'beat music' because of the strong repetitive rhythm of the music which proved ideal for rock 'n' roll dancing and jive.

I bought my first record player in 1957, a beige and red Dansette Junior single play model with three speeds to accommodate 78, 45 and 33rpm records, which I acquired second-hand for the princely sum of £2. From then on, I joined the groups of teenagers who spent most of every Saturday morning evaluating possible record purchases from the current Top Twenty in six small listening booths at Wolsey & Wolsey's electrical shop on King Street in Great Yarmouth. The first record that I bought was *Love is Strange* by Mickey and Sylvia and after that I purchased records at a rate of about one every fortnight. Initially my collection consisted only of rock 'n' roll and skiffle records, especially those recorded by Lonnie Donegan, the Everly Brothers and Buddy Holly and the Crickets but, by 1959, I was also adding jazz recordings, notably those performed by Chris Barber and the bowler-hatted Acker Bilk. In 1959, I enthused over Cliff Richard, Britain's curly-lipped answer to Elvis, and his ground-breaking recording of *Move it*. Cliff was at least British and original at a time when most rock 'n' roll artists were American and recordings by British singers were usually cover versions of American releases.

CHAPTER 5

ALL THAT JAZZ AND FOLK SONGS TOO

As well as listening to music, I enjoyed making music. In 1949 my parents bought a piano, a shiny new black upright piano that they placed in a prime position against the wall of our front room. During the 1950s most families considered a piano to be an essential possession, whether or not anyone in the house could play it. Many of my aunts and uncles owned a piano; mostly old upright pianos with yellowed keys that were out of tune and hardly ever touched. Mother was keen that I should learn to play our piano and, on my 10th birthday, arranged for me to have lessons from Miss Dyball, a music teacher from a neighbouring village. Despite some perseverance on her part, the lessons were a failure because no matter how hard I tried I could make little sense of musical notation. After a few months, Miss Dyball decided that I was un-teachable and the lessons ceased.

My interest in playing music was rekindled when I was given a harmonica as a 15th birthday present. Playing the harmonica proved not to be too difficult and very soon I was able to perform a number of recognisable popular tunes, much to my mother's delight. My uncle Billy Parnell was a talented harmonica player, as was his father before him, and he was often persuaded to entertain at our family parties. Under his tuition I learned the techniques of breath control, vamping and how to use my hands to vary the sound. He also introduced me to the popular Hohner range of harmonicas and I was soon the proud owner of two Hohner models, a chromatic harmonica with a slide button and a banana shaped Comet.

At about the same time, my Grandmother Miller gave me a rather battered ukulele-banjo and her collection of sheet music. Despite my inability to read music, I was able to teach myself how to play the ukulele because diagrams indicating the finger positions required for each chord were printed above the musical score. I eventually became quite competent at performing the songs from my grandmother's sheet music, which not only contained many jazzy numbers from the 1930s and '40s but also numerous George Formby hits including *Chinese Laundry Blues*, *I'm Leaning on a Lamp Post*, *Mister Wu*, *My Little Stick of Blackpool Rock*, *Ain't She Sweet* and *When I'm Cleaning Windows*. From then on I was also expected to do my musical bit at Christmas and at family parties. In 1957, armed with my harmonica and ukulele-banjo, I teamed up with a guitarist called Lenny to play skiffle music. Every weekend, accompanied by a tea chest bassist and

In 1958, I used all the money that I earned picking blackcurrants and working in the corn harvest to buy my first guitar.

washboard player, we made rhythmic noises in Lenny's front room, but our efforts failed to gain universal appreciation and we were never asked to perform in public.

In 1958 I used all the money that I had earned during the summer vacation, picking blackcurrants and beans and working in the corn harvest, to buy the instrument of the moment, an acoustic guitar. For most of the autumn I spent many long evenings in my bedroom with a Bert Weedon teach-yourself guitar manual, painfully learning finger positions and strumming out simple chord sequences. Within a few months I could play the chord sequences for many of the rock 'n' roll and skiffle numbers that were popular at that time with a teenage audience, which was not too difficult an accomplishment as many involved only four chord changes: C, A minor, F, and G7. All this was made easier by the fact that the fingering for the top four strings on the guitar was the same arrangement as that for the ukulele-banjo. I had merely to add fingering for the other two strings.

By the time I began my university course I considered myself to be a proficient guitarist and versatile musician. Among the residents of Southmeade was a second year mathematics student called Dave Cousins. Dave, a ginger haired young man with a stubbly beard, turned out to be a guitarist of national standing who was proficient in all styles of folk music, especially the songs of Woodie Guthrie, which he played on his battered acoustic Gretsch guitar. It was no surprise to me when I later discovered that Dave had embarked on a career in music after leaving university and eventually progressed to become the leader of a popular chart-topping band called The Strawbs. Many long evenings at Southmeade were spent playing with, listening to and learning from Dave's incredible guitar skills. My guitar playing was simply naïve by comparison. Under Dave's guidance, together with long hours of practice when I should have been studying, I successfully developed various techniques for playing the guitar, mainly finger-picking methods that included claw-hammer, slide and scratch. It was Dave who introduced me not only to the songs of Woodie Guthrie but also to the earthy music of numerous American folk and blues legends including Big Bill Broonzy, Muddy Waters, Sonny Terry, Brownie Magee, Howling Wolf and Hudie Ledbetter (better known as Leadbelly), music that also inspired many of the emerging rock 'n' roll artists of the 1950s and early 1960s.

In 1959, jazz rather than rock 'n' roll was the most acceptable form of popular music among Leicester University students, as it was in most universities. After looking through my collection of jazz records, Dave suggested that I might enjoy Club 57, a Sunday afternoon jazz club held at a dancing school above Burton's clothing shop near to the Clock Tower in Leicester's city centre. Intrigued by the thought of jazz on a Sunday afternoon, I travelled with Dave by bus into Leicester and climbed the 30 or more stairs to the top floor of a black and white building in Church Gate, on the corner of Church Street and High Street, close to the Clock Tower, where the sound of music was percolating from the premises of the Granby Dance Studios. Club 57 was a jazz club run mainly by students for students and I soon recognised some familiar faces both

Sunday jazz sessions at Club 57 were held in the Granby Dance Studios on the top floor above Burton's tailoring premises in Leicester's city centre. (by permission of the Record Office for Leicestershire, Leicester and Rutland)

on and off the stage. The band was a traditional jazz band consisting of trumpet, clarinet, trombone, banjo, bass and drums, and was drawn from students at the university and the Leicester Art and Tech. On trumpet and leader of the group was the unmistakable Pete Treger, the chairman of the university's Entertainments Committee, complete with his black beard and long wavy hair. As a ukulele-banjo player I was particularly fascinated by the band's banjoist, Phil Ward, a student from the Art and Tech who impressed me not only with his superb banjo playing technique but also because he wore long black buckled boots under the narrow bottomed trousers of his neatly pressed suit. More than anything, I coveted those boots.

Being a competent and enthusiastic dancer, I quickly overcame my initial self-consciousness and introduced myself to several potential dancing partners. I soon discovered Mavis and Gill, two third year university students, who were both excellent dancers and from then on I looked forward to meeting them every Sunday at the club to dance until we were exhausted. Gill was a conventional rock 'n' roll style dancer but Mavis taught me various versions of American jazz-style jive, including skip and slow jive, and was a real delight to dance with. Sunday afternoons were spent happily bouncing on the sprung floor of the dancing school amid a flurry of twirling skirts, petticoats, colourful knickers and stockings held up by suspenders. Mavis and Gill were avid fans of both modern and traditional jazz, while I simply preferred traditional jazz as, in my mind, it was dance music. On Thursday 22 October 1959, the three of us went to see the 72-year-old jazz legend, Kid Ory, perform with his Creole Jazz Band at the De Montfort Hall, Leicester's premier concert venue, ably supported by the excellent Terry Lightfoot and his New Orleans Jazz Band. Soon afterwards, in an

attempt to improve my appreciation for modern jazz, Mavis and Gill bought me a ticket for a concert by the Modern Jazz Quartet (the MJQ), also at the De Montfort Hall. I would never have considered buying such a ticket for myself. Despite their enthusiasm and encouragement, I was never able to appreciate or understand modern jazz.

Friday nights at the university were always the time for jazz at the Cellar Club. Because he was a jazz performer and music fanatic,

Kid Ory at the De Montfort Hall.

Jazz was popular with students.

Pete Treger had negotiated for the use of a cellar in the basement of the Percy Gee as the location for a jazz club where the university jazz band and invited bands from other universities and colleges in the Midlands could practice and play. It was at the Cellar Club where I

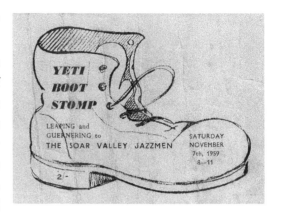

first met Spencer Davis when he was performing at the club as a member of a band from Birmingham University. Entered through a door at the end of a sloping walkway to the rear of the Percy Gee Building, the Cellar Club was held in a large, square, dimly lit, low-ceilinged and windowless room where, every Friday, the atmosphere was thick with dust, cigarette smoke and the smell of sweat, and every available space was occupied by reclining bodies and jiving couples. Leicester's own jazz band was a curious mixture of some very good and some not so competent musicians. In the smoky atmosphere of the Cellar Club, their music was rhythmic and provided the ideal beat for dancing. Despite their best efforts, at an inter-university jazz competition held at Bristol University in January 1960 their limitations were displayed for all to see when, during their competition piece, the clarinettist performed with an out of tune instrument and the drummer's kit fell apart. Nevertheless, we gave them full and rowdy support even though there was demonstrably little hope of success.

The Friday night Cellar Club provided an ideal location for meeting new female friends. My failure with Jean apart, I found little difficulty in finding girlfriends. At 19 years of age I was at my best. A fit and healthy young male, I weighed 11st 4lb and had well-toned muscles, the result of hard physical work and regular sport during my youth in the village of Rollesby. The deprivations of university life had not yet taken their toll. Despite a lack of confidence in the presence of the opposite sex, girlfriends came and went with monotonous regularity, some with much regret as was the case with Joanna.

During my first year at university there was little opportunity to play rock 'n' roll and so I developed my guitar skills by playing folk music and, from 1961, singing and performing at meetings of the university's Folk Song Society. Following the popularity of skiffle in the late 1950s, an interest in all kinds of folk music had undergone a revival. The Leicester University Folk Song Society was established in October 1961 and its members included many talented singers including Roy Bailey, Bob Hallum and Rod

Davies. Every week, the society met in a small back room at the Percy Gee to play, share ideas and learn new songs. The music played was a curious mixture of skiffle numbers, traditional British folk songs, ballads and sea shanties, and American folk, country and blues. Occasionally, guests from the city and other universities were invited to perform at club meetings. Spencer Davis' past links with the university ensured that he was a regular and much lauded visitor to the club, where he normally played blues music on his 12-string guitar while smoking rolled-up cigarettes made with brown liquorice-flavoured paper.

Tonight.
This Union's Folk Club.
SING OUT.
Starring
BAILEY, HALLUM, FRANKLIN, ROBINSON, MENDUM, DEAR,
MILLER and YOU.
When the Folk Club was started three weeks ago, the critics praised it to the skies. Roy Bailey's performance last week was the best thing he has ever done. For sheer entertainment value, this club is a winner. If you miss it this week you will be kicking yourself for a long time.
SO WHY NOT COME ALONG TONIGHT IN THE COUNCIL ROOM AT
7.30.
When the Folk Club presents
SING OUT.

Copy of a coffee bar hand-out, October 1961

By 1962, the Leicester University Folk Song Society had become an extremely popular and well supported club and attracted many local and national guest performers including Harvey Tucker, Geoff Halford, Sandra Bent, Christina Main, Charlie Crabtree, Bob Dubley, Mark Newman, Val Turbard and Russ Merryfield. On Friday 1 March 1963 The Folk Song Society organised a well-attended inter-university folk festival under the title of *A Grand Folk Hootenanny*, hosted by my student friend and fellow folk singer Rod Davies, featuring Spencer Davis and many of the above-named singers.

Before university, my guitar repertoire consisted mostly of current popular songs, mainly rock 'n' roll and skiffle numbers. I strummed and sung my own versions of Lonnie Donegan's hit songs *Rock Island Line*, *'Puttin' on the Style*, *Cumberland Gap* and *The Battle of New Orleans*, and Nancy Whiskey's ever popular *Freight Train*, as well as many

The Leicester University Cellar Jazz Club was held in a dusty and airless cellar to the rear of the Percy Gee Building. Every Friday, numerous students crammed into the cellar to dance, jostle and sweat to the sound of jazz. (Leicester Mercury Media Group)

contemporary rock 'n' roll numbers, particularly those recorded by Buddy Holly and the Crickets including *That'll be the Day*, *Peggy Sue*, *Oh! Boy*, *Rave On*, and the Everly Brothers versions of *Wake up Little Susie*, *Bye-bye Love*, *Poor Jenny* and *Till I Kissed You*, sometimes with Lenny's village skiffle band but mostly for my own amusement. At university I became especially competent at playing 12-bar blues which became my signature musical style at every folk club meeting; a style that I developed partly through my association with Dave Cousins and partly through a growing interest in American folk and blues music. My repertoire expanded gradually to include many Woodie Guthrie songs and Chicago-style blues numbers, especially up-beat bluesy versions of *San Francisco Bay Blues*, *This Land was Meant for You and Me*, *New York Town Blues*, *Good Morning Blues*, *The Midnight Special*, *Down by the Riverside*, *House of the Rising Sun*, *St James' Infirmary Blues* and many others, as well as novelty songs such as *The Foggy-Foggy Dew* and *The Hermit*.

The University's jazz band frequently gave impromptu performances on the campus. Some students listened while others jived. (R. Davies)

The social highlight of the university year was the spring term RAG week (Raising and Giving), seven or more days of energetic and often idiotic activities aimed at raising money for good causes. It was also the week that provided the last real opportunity for students to enjoy themselves before they had to settle down to hard work and revision for the end of year examinations. The theme for the 1960 RAG week was 'Age', chosen because most of the money raised was to be allocated for the purchase of a house in Severn Street, Leicester to be used as a university-managed residence for old people. Of the many events, the most popular were the pram race, where teams of relay runners from Leicester's many colleges and societies raced each other overnight while pushing a pram from London's Leicester Square to the Leicester Clock Tower, and the Saturday RAG Day, when garishly dressed students descended on the city to sell the RAG magazine, *Lucifer*, and to take part in a carnival procession through the centre of town. Traditionally, a float containing the Leicester RAG Queen was located at the front of the procession. 1960 was the year in which the RAG Committee broke with tradition and selected a RAG Queen from Leicester's student and nursing population rather than inviting a guest representative from a national bathing beauty competition. Despite the fact that bathing costumes were optional, it was some years before the concept of the traditional beauty contest died out. Miss

The Leicester University Athletic Club's entry to the 1960 RAG Pram Race. (R. Davies).

Running while pushing a pram from London to Leicester in front of the team coach was not without its perils. (R. Davies)

Margaret Danik, who was studying Architecture at the Leicester Art and Tech, was eventually selected as the 1960 Rag Queen and took pride of place at the head of the Saturday carnival procession; university undergraduates Judith Athill, Jan Lane and Marian Stuart were the Rag Queens of 1961, 1962 and 1963.

As part of Southmeade's involvement in RAG, Dave Cousins suggested that we should make a contribution to '*Madragal*', the

I played my ukulele-banjo in a makeshift jazz band on the back of a lorry in the 1961 RAG Carnival procession.

The cast of the 1960 Rag Revue, Madragal.

1960 Leicester University and Colleges' RAG revue, a music hall-style entertainment performed by students and open to the public, that was to be held on the Wednesday and Thursday of RAG week, 9 and 10 March, at Leicester's Corn Exchange in the market square. We eventually decided to enter a comedy sketch entitled *Crumbeat*, intended as a parody of the BBC television's popular rock 'n' roll programme, *Drumbeat*. Guitarists from the university's jazz band and folk club were invited by Dave to perform in the sketch as the members of a rock 'n' roll group. To enhance the sound from their acoustic guitars, students from the physics department designed and made amplification equipment with pick-ups (small microphones) which they screwed across the sound holes of each guitar. Two singers from Southmeade were eventually auditioned, selected and given appropriate stage names – Mike 'Vince' Minto and myself as the character 'Husky' Dusty Miller.

The revue itself was a mixture of good, bad and downright juvenile items which appeared, nevertheless, to go down reasonably well with the paying audience. The main visual attraction, particularly for the male members of the cast, was a modern dance troupe of scantily clad young ladies from the Scraptoft Teacher Training College. The finale of the evening was our musical offering, which was intended primarily to be a

Colin Coles and Dave Cousins rocking it up in Crumbeat.

comedy item. My contribution was a rather risqué version of Cliff Richards' current 1960 hit recording, *A Voice in the Wilderness*, sung while performing a number of suggestive contortions over the stage. Unfortunately, the singing and playing were considered so good that nobody laughed and we were immediately inundated with requests for bookings, including guest spots at 'Rock at the Troc', a rock 'n' roll concert the next evening in Leicester's Trocadero Ballroom, and at the Saturday RAG Hop in the Newark Drill Hall. For me, the most rewarding outcome was an invitation to attend a party organised by the RAG committee, those colourful characters that I so admired. I had made it, if not yet as a full member; at last I had been recognised by the in-crowd.

Despite this obvious success, my delight was somewhat muted as not everything that occurred during RAG week was to my credit. The dance troupe appearing in the RAG Revue was such a

A Voice in the Wilderness; my one and only attempt to be a rock singer.

L.U.C.R.C. *present*

MADRAGAL

At the CORN EXCHANGE, LEICESTER, MARCH 9th and 10th, 1960.

Members of the Company

MIKE JUDGE	ALAN POWELL	DAVE HORNE
MIKE McGOWAN	DAVE WILLIAMS	BERYL GLEDHILL
PETE NEWTON	JOSE WOODWARD	MARY LAMBERT
DENIS LEROY	ANNE WOOD	DUSTY MILLER
WAL PEARSON	CAROL PATTINSON	VINCE MINTO
BRENDA NASH	MIKE FENTIMAN	BRUCE EDGINGTON
PETE BULLOCK	PETE TREGER	DENNIS HOUSE
JUNE MASSEY	LIZ WATCHORN	DAVE CHALLIS
DAVE COUSINS	FRANK STARKEY	PAT SHARP
FRED COMBLEY	MALCOLM WOOLRIDGE	JANET LANE
JIM MARCHANT	DICK WHYARD	PETE HAWKINS
SID KENNINGHAM	ANDY WRAY	RUDKIN TURNER
DOREEN NEWTON		COLIN COLES

Ladies of the Chorus

Miss ANDREWS	Miss JOHNSON	Miss SQUIRES
„ ASH	„ MAXWELL	„ WILKINSON
„ BURBIDGE	„ ROBERTSON	„ WILLIAMS

Acknowledgments to
INTERVAL PIANIST : GRAHAM SMITHERS
MEMBERS OF THE PIT ORCHESTRA

Props and Costumes gathered by
Miss JOAN WIGHAM

Sound and Lights
Under scrutiny of Mr. BRANSTONE

Organised by Mr. HOPKINS

Secretary, Mr. JENKINS

Publicity : Mr. HOWE

Treasurer : Mr. SMITH

THANKS TO TYPISTS

SUPPORT RAG WEEK

RAG DAY, SATURDAY, MARCH 12th.

Madragal at the Corn Exchange.

MADRAGAL

AN EVENING'S DIVERTISSEMENT IN THE CORN EXCHANGE

The Company is not limited   *The Treasurer is still missing*

Dances were arranged by Freda Staire   Chef d'Orchestre M. Phillipe Harben

ORCHESTRA OF 45 PERFORMERS (Some with instruments)

(1)	Musical Introduction . . . THE LEICESTER SQUARE . . . . Strict tempo
(2)	A Historical Panorama **The Growth of Leicester** Members of the Company
(3)	A ROMANTIC DRAMA OF QUESTIONABLE AUTHENTICITY **FAMILY TIES (or a Knotty Problem)** *PERSONAL APPEARANCE OF SIR J. JASPER in the part in which his Father earned so much fame.*
(4)	*Chanson—niers de la gutter* **MINSTRELS PARISIENS** *dans leurs creations originales*
(5)	WE HAVE PLEASURE IN ANNOUNCING THE NON-APPEARANCE OF THE **FRANK BONHAIRE TROUPE OF ACROBATS** Instead our interviewer will speak to two old soldiers
(6)	**SITTING THIS ONE OUT (Backside Story)** *AN ENTHRALLING DRAMA OF GREAT PASSIONS AND FANTASTIC EXCITEMENTS IN THE MYSTERIOUS WORLD OF THE PALAIS-DE-DANSE* Presented by courtesy of the Enid Blyton " Fair to Fairies " League of Playmates.
(7)	**LAMENT** A Melancholy ballad for two voices *Performed reluctantly*
(8)	**The one and only WILFRED PUCKLES with his resident Company** " Bringing the People to the people "
(9)	**THE ELAGANTINE TROUPE** **Featuring the ladies of the Chorus**
	Interlude of ten minutes in which the audience is invited to participate
(10)	**RE-INTRODUCTION** **Sexy Rexy** A song of doubtful virtue by an artiste of great merit
(11)	An unsuccessful monologue "The Green Eye of the Little Yellow God" performed without musical accompaniment
(12)	*First appearance of a surprising Scientific Phenomenon* THE TIME MACHINE *Published in 1960 ; Reprinted 1909, and Revised in 1833.*
(13)	*Special and exclusive engagement of* **MR. PETER BULLOCK** in an entirely new series of his popular imitatic
(14)	THE CORN EXCHANGE a triology of humour in four parts
(15)	Re-appearance of the Minstrels Parisiens under the new title of MINSTRELS PARISIENS PLUS ONE *(minus helmets)*
(16)	**MOORES THE MERRIER** A TOPICAL DIVERSION NOT TO BE CONNECTED WITH THE SITUATION IN MATABELELAND OR THE AMERICAN COLONIES
(17)	**BEAU PEPYS** THE LIFE AND TIMES OF A DOCTOR'S WIFE FEATURING MEMBERS OF THE COMPANY. Any semblance to persons, known or unknown is regretted. *Portrayed without the kind permission of the Board of Guardians*
(18)	**For a Musical Finale in the Popular Idiom we proudly present** CRUMBEAT

PATRONS ARE REQUESTED NOT TO LEAVE THEIR HORSES IN THE FOYER UNATTENDED

The evening's entertainment.

visual sensation that some of the male performers from *Crumbeat* started a competition to see who would be the first to date Anne, the leader of the dancers. It was both my pleasure and my misfortune to be the winner of this competition. It was my pleasure as Anne was an extremely attractive and companionable young woman. It was also my misfortune because I was already dating Sandria, a student nurse from the Leicester Royal Infirmary, who I had met as a result of the retaliatory raid from Southmeade on the London Road nurses' home. It was my intention to go through with a date with the dancer, because that was a condition of the competition, but not to continue the liaison any further as I was well content with my nurse. My plans were upset entirely when both women informed me that they had acquired tickets for the RAG Hop and expected to see me there. My immediate hope of averting an embarrassing situation by avoiding the dance altogether was dashed when the cast of *Crumbeat* received the post-revue invitation to perform their revue act during an interval in the hop's proceedings, an invitation I could hardly refuse. My contingency plans were also upset when both women arrived at the hop at exactly the same time and my duplicity was revealed. Needless to say, my chances with both women evaporated immediately, and a fortnight of abject apologies and appeals to both Sandria and Anne fell on stony ground. My punishment was well deserved. It was vanity that had led to my dishonourable behaviour and it had not only caused hurt to two innocent and attractive young women but also to me. It taught me a salutary lesson and I resolved never to repeat this mistake again.

CHAPTER 6

INDEPENDENT LIVING

Once my first year examinations were over, I began collecting my possessions together and packing them away into my crimson trunk in preparation for leaving Southmeade House and returning home to Norfolk. The examinations had gone reasonably well, especially those for the Logic and Scientific Method module, and I was confident that I would be returning for the second year of the course. Most of my student colleagues were convinced that the first year examinations were regularly used by the university's staff to discard difficult or under-achieving students and that a pass would virtually guarantee the award of a degree. Eventually, my confidence was rewarded as a letter arrived confirming my success in the examinations. I had long decided not to re-apply for residence in Beaumont Hall but to seek accommodation in a student flat for the remainder of my course. Living in hall was far too restrictive and my flat dwelling friends appeared to have much more liberty to do as they pleased.

Tempted by the thought that a flat would provide freedom from rules, a venue for parties and a private place to entertain girlfriends, I made it known that I was seeking to become a flat dweller. As luck would have it Denis, one of my new university friends, told me that he was leaving his present accommodation and that I could take his place if I wished as he was about to move into another flat with his girlfriend. I considered the step that Denis and his partner were about to make to be excitingly modern and extremely bold for a young unmarried couple to take in 1960 and one that would doubtless have horrified not only my parents but probably his as well. Naturally I accepted his offer and it was agreed that, on my return, I would become one of the residents of a small student flat on East Park Road in Leicester.

I returned to Leicester at the end of September, in good time for the Integration Hop, an event not to miss now that I was an experienced second year student. Making my way to East Park Road, I found the house where I was to stay and with some trepidation, I rang the bell because I didn't have a key. My new residence at number 434 East Park Road was a large Victorian terraced house close to the Evington Road junction that had been divided into separate apartments, one on each of its three floors, with the top two let as student flats. The first floor apartment, consisting of lounge, twin bedroom, bathroom, separate toilet and kitchen, was the residence of Sheila and Marjory, two women students from the Scraptoft Teacher Training College.

My new flat was on the top floor and consisted of just two small rooms, a lounge and a kitchen-diner, which I shared with John, who was also a trainee teacher at Scraptoft.

At registration for my second year in the General Science degree, I confirmed the selection of Pure Mathematics as my main subject for the remaining years of the course, but I was having great difficulty in deciding on the two additional modules required for that year. I had not enjoyed Applied Mathematics and was determined not to include Physics under any circumstances. With two other like-minded companions, we successfully persuaded Mr Harré to offer an advanced course in Logic and Scientific Method for the coming year. As there were only three students in this spur-of-the-moment module, it was subsequently taught through tutorials and directed self-study, a method that suited my increasingly chaotic lifestyle. Failing to find an appropriate module to match those that I had already chosen, I finally opted for a course in British Archaeology, a subject of which I had no previous knowledge other than a general interest in the television programme *Animal, Vegetable, Mineral*, a popular quiz game of the late 1950s in which eminent archaeologists and historians were challenged to identify artefacts drawn from various British museums. I quite fancied myself as an eccentric successor to the programme's resident expert, the charismatic archaeologist, Professor Mortimer Wheeler.

The flat I shared with John at 434 East Park Road was comfortable but basic. There was no bathroom, so we washed in the kitchen sink, except on Sundays when we were permitted to use Sheila and Marjory's bathroom downstairs. We also shared the women's toilet, which was also located on the first floor. The basic kitchen-diner was furnished with a table, two chairs and a small cooker with an oven and four rings, and contained two small free-standing cupboards for storing cooking utensils, crockery and foodstuffs, and a walk-in cupboard for brushes, mops, an electric iron, ironing board and a Ewbank carpet sweeper. Hot water was provided by a small electric heater above the kitchen sink. Electricity came via a shilling meter housed in the hall on the ground floor. Cooking utensils, crockery and cutlery were limited, but had been supplemented by many of the flat's previous occupants with numerous illegal acquisitions taken from the Percy Gee coffee bar and various local restaurants, cafés and public houses.

In the lounge there was a sideboard under the single large window, a studio-couch which was unfolded each night to provide two single beds, a coffee table and two other chairs. A walk-in wardrobe provided the space for storing bedding and clothes. As there was no central heating, the only sources of warmth were a small open fire in the lounge and a portable single barred electric heater. Coal for the fire was purchased in bags from a local hardware shop and stored in a shed in the backyard. The kitchen had no fireplace and was, therefore, used as little as possible during the winter when it was usually freezing cold. The only luxury was a telephone in the downstairs hall which we were allowed to use for both incoming and outgoing calls, a bonus for me as my parents did not own a telephone until the late 1960s. An honesty box was placed beside the telephone for payments for outgoing calls. The owner of the house, an elderly bed-ridden lady who was looked after by a daily housekeeper, lived on the ground floor.

On my arrival at 434 East Park Road, it immediately became clear that living in a flat was not going to be as easy as I had expected. Like many young men of that time, I was ill-prepared in every way for looking after myself on a daily basis; at home, my mother had done everything for my father and me, while in hall most of my needs had been catered for as part of a residential package. I arrived at the flat equipped only with my guitar, a ukulele-banjo, my crimson trunk filled with books, toiletries, and clothes, and my collection of jazz recordings. I left my bicycle at Beaumont, never to be seen again.

At bedtime on my first evening at the flat, John asked where I had put my bedding. What bedding? I hadn't thought to provide myself with any bedding. John had sheets, blankets and a pillow for himself, but no spares at all to lend me. Eventually we found in the back of the lounge cupboard an old, grubby and somewhat smelly sleeping bag that John had used many years before while Youth Hostelling around the country. This bag became my night-time bedding not just for the one night but for the whole of my year-long stay at East Park Road. I became so used to sleeping without a pillow that it is still difficult for me now to sleep with my head propped up high.

Cooking was a mystery to me. My mother cooked all my food at home, usually from fresh ingredients. Neither my father nor I needed or were even encouraged to develop our cooking abilities beyond acquiring some basic survival skills for the odd occasions when my mother was ill, working, or away on a day trip with the Rollesby Women's Club. In her absence, we normally bought fish and chips from a shop in a nearby village, although my father occasionally boiled large Spanish onions which he ate covered with pepper. I arrived at East Park Road with little experience of cooking, other than knowing how to boil an egg and make porridge and custard. Not that I felt the need to improve my skills much further. On weekdays, I bought an evening meal from the restaurant in the Percy Gee and a salad or ham roll from the coffee bar at lunchtime. If I had sufficient capital, I used various local cafés and restaurants for my meals at weekends. When money was short, a chocolate bar often sufficed for lunch and, after a marked improvement in my expertise with a frying pan, sausages, egg and fried onions or a plate of Birds Eye fish fingers for my Sunday dinner, but occasionally I went without. I ceased making porridge when I suspected that John had been boiling his vests and underpants in the only saucepan.

I was not alone in my culinary ignorance. Like many young men of my generation, I regarded cooking as a woman's responsibility and had made little attempt to redress this ignorance. For her part, my mother happily assumed that it was her duty to cater for all my domestic needs when I was at home, a duty that she expected to continue until I married. Inevitably, many Students' Union officials were concerned by the lack of basic catering knowledge among students living in flats, especially young male students. In an attempt to rectify their ignorance, simple, quick, cheap, nutritious and easy-to-cook recipes with a minimum of ingredients were regularly published in the Leicester student newspaper, *Ripple*. Not that I was in any way tempted to try them as they always sounded unappetising and inedible. *Ripple*, the fortnightly newspaper of the Leicester University Students' Union, was first published on 10 December 1957 to disseminate Union news, information about student activities, useful tips on how to cope away from home and to provide a mouthpiece for student opinion. It replaced an earlier news-sheet *Wave*, which was allegedly the brainchild of Leicester alumnus, Malcolm Bradbury, author of the novel *Eating People is Wrong*.

Kasbah Hash

Melt about four tablespoonful of butter or margarine in a frying pan. Cut up an onion, add a cube of Oxo and a heaped dessertspoonful of curry powder. Throw in a dessertspoonful of marmalade and practically anything else you have in the house, raisins, nuts, apples, rind of lemon or orange (or both). If you haven't, a dash of lemon juice will do. When the onion is brown, add the contents of a tin of corned beef. Fry until the corned beef is cooked through and then serve. The whole dish should not take more than 15 minutes to make from start to finish.

The Ripple Recipe, *Ripple*, 6 November 1959

Cleanliness was a problem at our flat. Personal hygiene was difficult to maintain, confined as it was to washing daily in the kitchen sink and bathing once a week, but washing our bedding and clothes was an even greater nightmare. Coin-operated launderettes were beginning to appear in Leicester, but none was conveniently located for John or me to use, and private laundries were far too expensive for cash-strapped students. Providing that the weather was fine, John, Sheila and Marjory washed their sheets once a week in the bath. Luckily, my sleeping bag did not need laundering, although by the end of the year it smelled rather rank. Washing clothes in the sink was not ideal and the long trek down two flights of stairs and out to the back yard to use the one communal linen line was a great deterrent. Inevitably, my clothes were worn for as long as possible, even shirts and underwear, and I have no doubt that I was frequently unkempt and smelly. My eventual solution to this problem was quite simple. I had just discovered the joys of hitchhiking which, in the 1950s and early 1960s, was a relatively quick, cheap and convenient way for students and members of the armed forces to travel around the country. Once I had plucked up the courage, I found that it was relatively easy to hitchhike the 120 miles along the A47 between Leicester and my home in Norfolk, with a journey time averaging between four to six hours. So at least twice every term, I packed my dirty washing into the ex-army kitbag that I had bought at an Army and Navy Stores and hitchhiked home so that my mother could launder and iron my clothes and, at the same time, I could enjoy the benefits of mother's home-cooking. The journey was best accomplished during the working week and that involved missing lectures. Luckily, Jean was always on hand to sign my name on the register and make excellent notes for me to copy.

John, my new flatmate at East Park Road, was a student teacher in his final year at the Scraptoft Teacher Training College and, being a year or so older than me, was far more confident and worldly wise. Despite a few initial teething problems in our relationship, we soon became great friends and, with John's help and guidance, I became quite used to the daily routine of living in our small, cramped accommodation. A weekly rota for the essential chores was drawn up: dusting and cleaning, buying the coffee, clearing, relaying and lighting the fire, emptying the bins and filling the coal bucket. A few house rules were established, the most important of which was that if either of us was entertaining a girlfriend in the flat then we should not be disturbed by the other. Luckily, Sheila and Marjory in the flat below were quite content for their lounge sofa to be used occasionally as a spare bed. On one occasion, I was forced to share the sofa with one of these young women when her flatmate was also entertaining a boyfriend.

John was a particularly confident and self-assured 21-year-old, undoubtedly the result of his upbringing. His brothers were successful professionals and his father held an eminent position in the Church of England. John revelled in the idea that they considered him to be the black sheep of the family because of his strongly held socialist views. John had four passions that dominated his life: jazz, politics, women and teaching. By the end of my time with John at East Park Road, I had been extensively tutored in every aspect of all four.

John was an extremely competent trumpet player and had formed a jazz band that played regularly at university and college dances. Before beginning his course at Scraptoft, he had played trumpet with Doug Richford's London Jazzmen before giving way to Nat Gonella and then, for a short while, with the popular Cy Laurie's Jazz Band. At every available opportunity morning, noon and night, jazz music blared out from John's record player. His collection of old 78 recordings and contemporary LPs occupied most of the cupboard space in our lounge sideboard. My collection was pathetic by comparison, consisting mainly of those British revivalist jazz bands of the 1950s and early 1960s that had become popular with young people: Acker Bilk, Ken Colyer, Chris Barber, Kenny Ball, The Temperance Seven and their like. John, on the other hand, was a fan of traditional pre-World War Two New Orleans and Chicago based jazz, particularly that played by King Oliver's Creole Jazz Band, the Original Dixieland Jazz Band and Louis Armstrong's Hot Five and Hot Seven, but his pride and joy was a large collection of 78rpm records featuring the jazz pianist Jelly Roll Morton and his Red Hot Peppers. Through John's tuition, my introduction to this early and essentially black American music was a revelation and a joy.

When we were not listening to jazz, we played jazz, John on his trumpet and me accompanying on my guitar or ukulele-banjo. Through playing with John I became familiar with most of the traditional jazz classics and memorised the chord sequences for many of them. We were often joined by other student musicians and jam sessions were a regular feature of daily life at East Park Road. Our top flat frequently resonated with the strains of *When the Saints Go Marchin' In*, *Tiger Rag*, *Down by the Riverside*, *Basin Street Blues*

and many other rousing jazz compositions. I became sufficiently competent to deputise, albeit badly, for his band's banjo player on a few occasions when he was unavailable to play at their gigs. Sunday mornings were especially enjoyable because we were visited by many of John's musician friends and

John with Phil Ward. John and his trumpet were rarely parted. (R. Davies)

other jazz-loving acquaintances to drink coffee, listen to records and play music. Some of our visitors were clearly well-to-do and arrived outside our flat in well-polished sports cars. Without doubt, jazz rather than rock 'n' roll was the preferred music of most middle-class young people as well as students. Afterwards, we were often taken for a Sunday car ride and treated to lunch at a Leicestershire country inn.

John's other great passion was politics, in particular socialist politics and the fortunes of the British Labour Party. Like many young people of the late 1950s and early 1960s, I had little interest in British party politics. At 16, I knew that the Conservatives were in power but I had little idea about the principles they represented or their party manifesto. I understood that my parents voted Conservative because they believed that the Conservatives best represented the views of country folk, even working-class country folk, but how or why they did so was a mystery to me and, most probably, to my parents as well. I lacked interest because, as a teenager, I was unable to vote and would not be eligible to do so until I reached the age of 21. At Great Yarmouth Grammar School national politics were rarely discussed, or at least not with the science section of the sixth form. Those of us who had chosen to take the scientific path were certainly more ignorant of politics and national affairs than those in the arts sixth, because science orientated students were forced to drop history as a subject after the third year. This certainly compounded my ignorance, because politics and history seem to be inextricably linked. What little knowledge I had of national and international affairs was gleaned from reading newspapers and listening to the radio, and, as my parents normally read the *Daily Express*, it was knowledge that had a definite right wing bias.

My interest in international affairs was limited to concerns about the various conflicts that occurred around the world during the 1950s: the UN action in Korea, the popular uprisings in Cyprus, Kenya and Malaya, as well as the consequences of the debacle of Suez. My concerns were heightened by the prospect that, at 18, I would become eligible for 18 months of National Service in the armed forces. In the early 1950s, my cousin Mary's husband, Tommy, saw active service in Korea during his time on National Service with the Royal Marines, a traumatic experience that gave him nightmares on his return. By the late 1950s, my cousins Francis and Michael were also serving their time in the forces as were many of my Norfolk friends, one of whom returned from Cyprus with a bullet wound to his leg, the result of an accidental discharge of a rifle rather than from any action by an enemy. Despite the fact that my friend's wound was accidental, it clearly brought home to me the potential dangers that were involved in National Service. But, my worries were unfounded, because by the time I had completed my university course in 1962 and became available for the 'call-up', National Service had been abolished. On the wider issues, like most of my friends I was terrified by the thought of a nuclear war with Russia, a distinct possibility in the 1950s and early 1960s, and the fact that a four-minute warning could herald imminent destruction. A fear that was magnified many times in my mind by the training in post-nuclear war survival techniques that my parents received as members of Britain's Civil Defence Corps. The creation and testing of bigger and more powerful bombs by all four of the major powers did little to ease my fears. Films showing the effects of the relatively small Atomic bombs dropped on Hiroshima and Nagasaki by the Allies during the war with Japan demonstrated effectively the certain outcome of any such conflict. I remember distinctly my amazed reaction when one of my friends said that, if war broke out, he would rather be vaporised in the centre of an atomic blast than survive to suffer the effects of radiation.

Unlike me, my flatmate John was a keen student of international politics. His leisure-time reading consisted almost exclusively of books relating to socialism, the Labour party and the Russian Revolution. John undoubtedly considered me to be politically naïve and frequently engaged me in earnest discussions. All too quickly I acquired enough knowledge of socialist history and theory to hold my own in any Junior Common Room debate. I became well versed in the history and policies of the British Labour Party, the ideas of Marx and Engels and the Communist Party Manifesto, and of the life of Lenin, the Bolsheviks and the history of the Russian Revolution. In many ways, the ideas that arose from my discussions at the university and with John in our East Park Road flat appealed very much to my youthful idealism. Yet, the pages of *Ripple* clearly indicated that not everybody at the university was ready and willing to challenge the status quo or to adopt socialist values.

A little addition to the stew of socialism that continues to bubble here

Those children dressed in Blue are educated to the third 'R' of Responsibility; whilst those poor little kids in Red are endowed with that third 'R' of Rights.

Leicester Diary, *Ripple*, 28 November 1959

Nevertheless, like my parents, I considered Russia to be the great modern threat and, despite its genuine appeal, I could not in any way reconcile the idealism of socialist theory with the cruel and expansionist dictatorship that I perceived to exist in communist Russia at that time. Neither could I forget the ruthless way in which the

Russian army had dealt with the popular uprisings in Hungary and Czechoslovakia during the mid-1950s. In spite of John's enthusiasm and commitment, I could not find it in myself to become passionately committed to politics of any persuasion, left, right or centre. I was clearly one of the apathetic student majority that the university's Socialist Society frequently complained about. I did mildly support multilateral nuclear disarmament but not unilateral disarmament. John supported the latter and was a keen member of the Campaign for Nuclear Disarmament.

The genuine fear of nuclear war resulted in the creation of the Campaign for Nuclear Disarmament (CND) in 1958, with John Collins, Canon of St Paul's Cathedral, as its Chairman and one of my heroes, the philosopher and mathematician Bertrand Russell, as its President. From 1959, CND was responsible for organising the annual Aldermaston March, taking over from the Committee for Direct Action, who organised the first march in 1958. While the figureheads of CND were writers, politicians, philosophers, eminent scientists and religious leaders, the ordinary membership was comprised mostly of young people, many of whom were students. So although the reason for the annual march was serious, it also became a festival for the young, with many jazz bands accompanying and entertaining the marchers as they wearily tramped from Aldermaston to the Trafalgar Square in London. John proudly wore their distinctive badge at all times on his jacket lapel, a small black and white badge with a design based on the semaphore signals for N and D inside a circle, and had taken part in the first march organised by CND in April 1959, no doubt accompanied by his trumpet.

Although it failed to achieve its aim of a ban on nuclear armaments, CND had a great influence on student thinking because its activities, especially the annual marches, demonstrated the ability of mass protest to influence opinions and to potentially change decisions, and was not just another excuse for an enjoyable jazz festival for the young. Two mass demonstrations had previously been successfully used to bring about positive change on the Leicester University campus. The first one took place in 1958 to protest about the poor quality of the meals and coffee served in the Percy Gee Students' Union Building. The second action was in 1959, my first year at the university, when the student body sought to overturn the decision by the University Senate to make the wearing of gowns at lectures compulsory. These successful non-violent actions were a gentle foretaste of the more serious and disruptive student protests that occurred at Leicester and many other universities during the late 1960s.

Where the opposite sex was concerned, John definitely had a penchant for the cultured middle-class variety. His confident manner and rugged good looks ensured that most of his girlfriends were the daughters of professional people and he had no qualms about escorting them to hunt balls and champagne parties dressed in a dinner jacket and bow tie, although he frequently remarked that his many girlfriends insisted on paying for their own tickets and often his as well. His conquests were numerous and, as a result, I was regularly forced to make use of Sheila and Marjory's lounge sofa. In discussions about sex, the issue of contraception invariably arose. 'If ever you run out of Johnnies, then there are spares in the cupboard', was his frequent sensible and friendly advice. Until then, the idea of possessing contraceptives 'just in case' had never entered my head. I was one of many young men who, at that time, were hoping for a sexual experience to happen but totally unprepared for one if it did.

Chapter 7

Understanding the facts of life

Like most young single men, my social life in the late 1950s and early 1960s was dominated by the search for that special female companion – my potential partner for life – and an insatiable curiosity regarding sex. Inevitably, both were inextricably linked and frequently confused. Lust was often mistaken for love and vice versa. It soon became clear to me that, while the attitudes and prejudices of incumbent society made the quest for an enduring partner difficult to accomplish, every effort was made to make experiences of sex even more difficult to fulfil. Nevertheless, once I had discovered the delights of having a girlfriend – the excitement of the pursuit, the anticipation of a first date and the eventual thrill of a kiss – it ensured that others came and went with some regularity. I revelled in the joys of having a special companion on my arm and the increased maturity that I experienced through her presence. I also discovered the pain and grief that often accompanied the ending of a relationship and, occasionally, the despair at being discarded for another.

Yet, despite my experiences with many girlfriends, it was painfully apparent that in most issues relating to sex I was dangerously ignorant. Luckily, before university and despite my best efforts, other than kissing and some inexpert fumbling in the dark, my practical experience of sex was nil. My theoretical knowledge of sex was also extremely inaccurate and unsafe, derived as it was from teenage gossip and some limited factual information acquired from lessons at school. I naively believed that sex was the ultimate goal of all close and committed male-female relationships and to do 'it' was its final fulfilment, although I was strongly conditioned by my parents to believe that 'it' might have to wait until marriage. In truth, I was not completely sure what 'it' was, what 'it' entailed or what its consequences were and 'it' remained a mystery for me until well after I had begun my studies at Leicester.

From an early age, I was well aware that boys and girls were different, and that those differences were for a purpose. However, every time I tried to initiate a conversation on the subject with my mother, she would round on me and proclaim 'That's dirty talk' or 'You'll find out when you're old enough'. Indeed, neither of my parents had any meaningful discussions with me regarding procreation or the problems associated with courtship and sex. On one memorable occasion, having caught sight of a diagram in my biology notebook, my mother exclaimed 'Well, at least I won't have to tell you about the facts of life'. What the renal system of a rabbit had to do with the facts of life I was not at all sure, but, true to her word, she never did. Neither were my parents keen for me to start dating girls. Until I was 16, they continually insisted that my education should take precedence over relationships with girls and they actively discouraged me from entering into any such associations. Having discovered that I had been seen in the village walking hand-in-hand with a female friend, my 1955 bonfire night conquest, I was strongly advised that I was too young to think of girls and that I should concentrate on my studies, good advice that I subsequently ignored.

By the time that I was 17, they finally accepted that I was old enough for a girlfriend and I was encouraged to bring my friends back home where they could be vetted and our activities strictly supervised. Whether by accident or design, young men and women were rarely left by themselves in the small and often overcrowded homes of the time. Although I had a bedroom of my own upstairs, containing my radio, record player and personal effects, my parents never considered it to be a proper place for entertaining friends, especially female friends. Other than visits to the cinema or to the dance hall, a walk in the countryside was the only opportunity we had to be free from their supervision. Even then, it was difficult to be away from the watchful eyes of other village adults who would often report back to my parents what they had seen. It was not easy to find a private place to be alone at a time when few young people had access to a motor car. While my parents eventually appeared happy for me to have a special female friend, every effort was made to condition me against experimenting with sex or treating the relationship as being anything other than temporary.

Despite my parents' best efforts in that respect, it was really a combination of the possible embarrassment at being found wanting by a potential partner, my ignorance of the techniques and processes involved and the fear for the possible consequences that were the greatest deterrents to any sexual adventures on my part. My only formal instruction about sex was a talk given in my fourth year at grammar school by the biology teacher on the topic of human reproduction, which was based on a film strip that consisted of about 20 or more pictures and diagrams. The first picture was of a man and a woman with a boy and a girl, all naked. Despite my careful scrutiny and that of all my classmates, the picture was taken at such a distance that it was not possible for us to see any of their intimate parts in any detail. The sex bit was dispensed with diagrammatically in the next two frames and added very little to my knowledge base, and the remainder of the film strip concentrated mainly on pregnancy and birth. Most of my actual sex instruction was delivered by older school colleagues and included many myths as well as some useful knowledge, although for an inexperienced youth it was difficult to judge which was which.

Pictures of nakedness were not commonplace and any that appeared were studied in detail. One sixth form pupil, a member of a local photographic society, had acquired a picture of a naked woman that had been taken in a life class. Using his society's photographic enlarger, he had produced a number of magnified photographs of certain areas of this woman's body which he proudly circulated among most of the senior school, although, during the enlargement process, the pictures had become so misty and indistinct that we were not at all sure what we were looking at. Masturbation, contraception, sexually transmitted diseases and homosexuality were never discussed either at home or in the lessons at school, and so I was totally ignorant where these issues were concerned. It was comforting to discover that most of my peer group were as ignorant as me, although we shared what knowledge we had between ourselves, no matter how inaccurate or ill-founded it might have been. At 16, we were all terrified by the thought that hairs might grow on the palms of our hands, or that we would become deaf, mentally unstable or acquire nasty red-rashes on our private parts as a result of personal sexual experimentation, fears that were often magnified in our minds by the jibes of the older and wiser members of the upper sixth.

Fear and ignorance were strong inhibiting factors to any sexual adventures. I was particularly fearful of getting caught in the act. I can remember cycling home from a village dance with one young woman who, when we stopped near to her house, appeared to be concerned that we might be discovered together despite the fact that nothing untoward was happening. She eventually told me that on a previous occasion she had been found in a compromising position with another young man by the local village policeman, who had threatened to tell her father if he caught her in a similar situation again. In the 1950s, most young women feared the wrath of their fathers and most fathers were highly protective where their daughters were concerned. Consequently, I arrived at university still sexually inexperienced. Despite my best efforts, at just 19 years of age I had still not 'done it', 'gone all the way' or 'reached base ten'. Base nine and a half maybe, but always, at the last minute, fear overcame lust in either my partner or me and abruptly terminated proceedings, both the fear of the unknown as well as the fear of its possible consequences. Not that my experience was unique. Many of my university friends were as equally uninitiated as me, although our numbers grew fewer as time passed by and the less supervised environment of a university campus facilitated greater experimentation within our personal relationships.

My mind was totally confused. At home, my parents considered that sex should wait until marriage and the possibility of sex before marriage was not entertained or discussed. For them, sexual activities outside marriage were dirty, irresponsible and entirely wicked. Inevitably, influenced by their views I considered sex to be the eventual glue of a long-established personal relationship with a partner who I knew and liked, even if I did not wish to wait until marriage before experiencing its pleasures. From the start, I was conditioned both at home and at school to believe that the primary, if not the only aim of sex was procreation and not recreation. Not that I adhered to this belief in any way, but I did hold the rather romantic view that sex expressed a commitment to a relationship, no matter whether that relationship proved to be temporary or enduring. Yet, for many of my male friends the quest for a sexual conquest was paramount, although for most of us it remained an unobtainable goal. I had a few friends in both rural Norfolk and urban Leicester whose sexual adventures were legendary and who moved from one partner to another without any intention of seeking a permanent relationship, but they were a minority. I was shocked when one of my university friends admitted that he sought nothing but sex from the women he dated and openly declared to them that this was his prime objective, sometimes at their first meeting. He also admitted that most of the women that he dated would not comply with his wishes, but it was the few who did that made his openness worthwhile. Even with a high failure rate, he accurately concluded that he was far more experienced in sexual matters than me. In my experience, it was not unusual for a first date to end with a handshake and not with a kiss and a cuddle, or anything more.

Inevitably, I was totally unprepared when, one evening at 434 East Park Road, it seemed likely that my time had finally arrived. With John's warnings about the need for contraception ringing in my ears – 'If ever you run out of Johnnies, then there are spares in the cupboard' – I sought out the important protective item. Unfortunately, John had failed to mention which cupboard. My female companion must have been totally bemused while she watched me ransack the broom cupboard in the kitchen, the wardrobe cupboard in our lounge and the drawers and cupboards in the sideboard. The fact that my search was unsuccessful did not really matter as the moment had long passed before I eventually returned to my partner, if indeed it had ever existed in the first place.

But as a result of this experience, I decided that I should act responsibly and equip myself in case a similar situation arose in the future. I was too embarrassed to approach the female counter assistants at the local chemist's shop, so I elected to visit a gentleman's hairdresser on Granby Street in order to have a badly needed haircut and to purchase a packet of condoms, or Johnnies as they were called at the time. When the time came, I paid for my haircut and, in a hushed voice, requested the sought-after package. Sensing my inexperience in these matters, with a smile on his face and in a voice loud enough to be heard by his waiting customers, the barber enquired, 'Large or small sir?' My response of 'Large' caused great hilarity among his clientele, a well-practised joke but one that I innocently fell for. When the long awaited and keenly anticipated moment finally arrived, I was still unprepared and the event, which was disappointingly over almost as soon as it began, was such an anticlimax as to make me wonder, albeit briefly, if the moment was really worth the long wait.

In the late 1950s and early 1960s, contraception was clearly a man's responsibility. The pill had yet to become freely available and the consequential sexual revolution of the late 1960s had yet to begin. The only secure course of action available to young single women was abstinence. Along with many of my contemporaries, contraception was a responsibility for which I was basically unprepared and sometimes misinformed. School tuition on the basics of human reproduction did not include any information about contraception and personal responsibilities. The subject of premarital sex and birth control was never addressed openly at home either, apart from a few oblique references and warnings. During my vacations from university, my mother frequently expressed the hope that I was not 'getting up to those things that some boys get up to when they are away from home'. Despite her fears, she did not consider contraceptive advice to be appropriate, despite a dire warning never to disgrace our family by bringing a pregnant girl back home if I did not wish to find the door shut in my face. Presumably she also considered abstinence to be the only proper course of action for an unmarried male.

So my only real source of useful and relevant information was from the more experienced members of my peer group, like John at East Park Road. The only person in my family ever to mention contraception was my Grandfather Miller who, one week before my wedding day, sent me a letter wishing me a happy future and advice concerning the contraceptive methods that he had used during his marriage, including a condom (which he referred to as a sheath), coitus interruptus, the rhythm method and non-penetrative sex – advice offered far too late to be of any practical use. He also concluded that as he and Grandmother Miller had had six children, none of these methods was fool proof. He then confessed that he had joined the army in 1910 not out of duty, patriotism or a lust for adventure but as a means of limiting the size of his family.

Towards the end of 1963, the Students' Union at Leicester was greatly disturbed by a request from the *Daily Mirror* to circulate among the general student body a questionnaire put together by the newspaper's 'agony aunt', Marjorie Proops, exploring the sexual attitudes and activities of students at university. The survey, as published in the February 1964 edition of *Ripple* asked:

Is promiscuity in your University or College at anything like the level reported by a Harvard psychiatrist that 'more than 50 per cent of college women had intercourse with students'.

If the answer is YES, please give possible reasons. If the answer is NO, at what level would you estimate promiscuity to exist?

Is there too much freedom and opportunity in your University or College for sexual activities?

Are promiscuous relationships more or less 'steady' – or is there a good deal of casual promiscuity?

Do girls seek illicit sexual activities? Or are the men mainly the pursuers?

Should University Authorities take on the responsibility of giving students 'emotional education'? If so, how?

Do students really want absolute freedom? Or would most prefer some sort of discipline? Would they resist regulations to restrict sexual activity?

Are students (presumably intellectually advanced) emotionally immature?

Do men students place any value at all on chastity? Would they expect it in the girls they marry?

Do students feel that pre-University schooling should provide wider and better sex instruction?

Do students consider parents' sex instruction generally adequate?

What are the penalties for being caught out in a promiscuous relationship in your University?

The SRC at Leicester concluded that it was in the interests of students not to respond as they believed strongly that the tenor of the questionnaire indicated that it was designed specifically to show that unacceptably promiscuous behaviour was rife within British universities. During my time in Leicester, student behaviour had changed and attitudes had become more liberal, but to suggest that students had become recklessly promiscuous would seem to be too extreme. Inevitably, in the confined society of a university or college with a population consisting mainly of intelligent and inquisitive young men and women between 18 and 25 years of age, most of whom were willing to challenge the norms of contemporary society, it was likely that many, if not most, were sexually active to some degree or another. Among my friends, consensual sex had become increasingly common and cohabitation was more frequent in 1964 than appeared to be the case when I arrived at Leicester in 1959, but these experiences were still mostly confined to students in long-term or potentially permanent relationships. Casual sex-for-sex-sake was still restricted to the over-publicised minority. Nevertheless, despite its obvious quest for sensational newsworthy material, the *Daily Mirror* questionnaire did accurately focus upon many of the issues that had confronted me during my formative years. It was not until the late 1960s that advances in contraception would enable the free-love aspirations of the 'make love not war' flower-power generation to become possible. Even as late as 1964, my memories of that time would suggest that for most young people outside of London the so-called sex-mad, drug-crazed swinging sixties did not exist. With a few exceptions, most of us were gently rocking rather than completely swinging to the beat.

CHAPTER 8

DANCING TO A LEICESTER BEAT

As a young man, my love of dancing not only ensured that was I becoming extremely competent at rock 'n' roll and jive, but I was also familiar with conventional ballroom dancing. At university, I readily slipped into a weekend routine that involved a quick drink or two in the students' bar to bolster up my courage, after which I joined my friends at the Saturday Hop in the Queen's Hall of the Percy Gee. Billed as the cheapest dance in Leicester, the hop attracted not only student dancers but also large numbers of the local youth, particularly young women in search of a student companion. For most of my undergraduate years, we danced the waltz, foxtrot and quickstep to music played by a traditional dance band. Regular performers at the hop were Dick Baker and his Band featuring Christine Owen, an attractive lady vocalist, and the locally popular Danny Rogers' Orchestra. Rock 'n' roll and jive were usually restricted to sessions

Students take a break from the Saturday dance. Smart suits and dresses were the order of the day in the early 1960s. (R. Davies)

during the interval when we danced to music from a gramophone or the occasional live group.

Meeting young Leicester women at the dance was a novel experience and one that occasionally developed into a longer term relationship. It was a firm belief among many of my contemporaries that these young local working women, especially those employed in the buoyant textile and shoe factories of Leicester, were not only sexually active but also awash with money and would happily spend it to obtain a student boyfriend, beliefs totally unsupported by any personal experience. At one Saturday dance, I met and eventually escorted home an attractive young woman from Oadby. On arriving at her home, I was invited into the kitchen for coffee where I was confronted by two unfriendly looking Alsatian dogs. I was warned not to make too much noise in case I should annoy the dogs or disturb her parents, who were watching television in the next room. It soon became clear to me that my new friend was intent on performing an intimate act on the kitchen table. Horrified by her forwardness as well as fearing an attack by the dogs or the unexpected appearance of her parents, in cowardly fashion I hastily made my excuses and fled. Luckily, I was such a disappointment that the young lady totally ignored me at the next Saturday dance.

During the week I often ventured into the centre of Leicester to attend midweek dances at the Palais de Danse on Humberstone Gate, a conventional ballroom with a stage for the band at one end of the dance floor, tables around the other three sides and a bar on the upstairs balcony. The resident band played all forms of music for dancing and even had a spot in the programme specifically designated for rock 'n' roll. For a while I made a great effort to dress properly for the occasion, like most young men in the early 1960s. My garish blue and red checked suit that my grandmother bought for my 16th birthday had at last been replaced by a more sombre charcoal-grey two piece, which became my usual dress not only for dancing but also for interviews and all other formal occasions; it even served eventually as my wedding suit. But formality was starting to ease and I often went dancing at the Palais dressed in cavalry twill or brown corduroy trousers, green shirt and a sports jacket.

My regular dance partner for most of the autumn of 1960 was Maria, a farmer's daughter from Enderby, whom I met every week at the Palais. Maria was a fun companion and a good ballroom dancer, but her conversation was limited to current teenage issues, scandal and tittle-tattle. Throughout the month of November, Maria slowly and systematically read her way through a newly-released paperback copy of *Lady Chatterley's Lover* by D.H. Lawrence, an interest that arose out of curiosity because of the adverse publicity the book had received as a result of the obscenity charge brought against the publisher, Penguin Books, and not for its literary content. She also bought a copy for me to read so that we could discuss the controversial sections of the book whenever we met. Despite her profound interest in its more explicit content, I could never persuade Maria to act out any of the situations described in the text.

Just before the Christmas vacation, I met Clare, a petite student of fashion from the Leicester Art and Tech. Clare's special subject was corsetry and she regularly squeezed her slender body into numerous flesh-restraining garments, some commercial and others of her own design, despite the fact that she was extremely thin. Holding Clare was like holding a Greek statue, everywhere was stiff and hard where it should have been soft and pliable. She was totally convinced that corsetry was an essential part of fashion and that it offered her a career opportunity for the future. My own opinion of corsetry was coloured by memories of the vast pink-coloured elastic, bone and wire contraptions that my mother wore under her dress for special occasions. I liked Clare and we spent many evenings together at dances and parties gyrating to the latest craze, the twist. The only down side to our association was that she lived in lodgings in a house just off the Uppingham Road, a good distance from my accommodation on East Park Road. On many evenings, after escorting Clare back to her residence on the last bus, I had to walk the two miles or more back to my flat. Thank goodness it was normally a safe but solitary walk, as Leicester's streets were virtually deserted after midnight in the early 1960s.

The Leicester College of Art and Technology (the Art and Tech) was an endless source of attractive girlfriends.

Clare was the bright 18-year-old daughter of a vicar and a self-confessed virgin, and she was determined to remain so until marriage, an objective that was not uncommon among many young women of that time. Despite the many intellectual and physical challenges that I brought to bear on her beliefs, it was a resolve that she maintained throughout all of our association. Clare believed strongly that men should be sexually experienced before marriage, but that all brides should be virgins. How this could be achieved, I was not at all sure. However, Clare insisted that there were sufficient prostitutes, delinquent girls with easy morals and bored housewives with tired husbands for this to fulfil the need. Indeed it was true that many of my experienced friends confessed that their first sexual encounters had been with young married women and, in one case, a not so young married woman. As one of my friends succinctly commented, casual relationships with married women were much safer because any accidental consequences could be blamed on the husband. Many also confessed, hypocritically, that they too hoped that their brides would be virgins.

My relationship with Clare ended abruptly, just at a point where it seemed to be thriving. After an exhilarating but exhausting evening dancing to the Cubanaires and the Temperance Seven at the 1961 Union Ball, Clare said that she was sad to think that our association would inevitably come to an end one day soon, because she was intent on a career in fashion and, as I was yet unqualified, I was clearly not in a position where I could make a commitment. Her comments reminded me of Joanna and the disappointment that I felt on that separation, and made me more determined that it would not happen again. I was still unused to young women who placed a career before partnership, which might have been unrealistic, but at the same time I was not prepared to embark emotionally on a relationship that had no possibility of a future.

For me, the second half of the 1961 spring term had a definite continental flavour. Since parting with Clare, I had spent much of my time in the company of a group of students from Denmark, Germany and Austria. Jazz at the Granby School of Dancing's Club 57 had become very popular with overseas students, most of who were on exchange study visits as part of their training, or working temporarily as domestics at various university and college halls of residence. My main interest focussed on Krista and Karin, twins from Austria, who were both jazz enthusiasts and good dancers. So identical were they that, until I knew them well, I was unsure which of them I was dating at any one time. After a Sunday afternoon dance session at Club 57, the three of us usually returned to 434 East Park Road to drink coffee and listen to jazz records, particularly their favourite recordings of *You're Driving Me Crazy* and *Pasadena* by the Temperance Seven, which we played time after time. They were especially delighted

Karin, Ingrid and Krista, continental friends from Club 57. Meeting students from other countries was a new and novel experience for me. (R. Davies)

when, after attending a concert given by the Temperance Seven at the De Montfort Hall, we arrived at a party where we were introduced to three members from the band, Paul McDowell, Cephas Howard and Alan Swainston Cooper.

Student life was not always without its perils, a fact that was clearly demonstrated when one of the regular female dancers at Club 57 suddenly failed to appear amid rumours that she was pregnant. It was also suggested that the man involved was married, but had raised enough money for her to have an abortion – a drastic, illegal and potentially hazardous solution to an awkward problem. I failed to establish the truth of the matter because she never returned again to Club 57. In the 1950s and early '60s, the fear of pregnancy and its consequences was a prime concern for young single women and a major deterrent to casual sex. Although sex between unmarried couples was not uncommon (a fact that was not lost on many young men, myself included) it usually took place between engaged couples or couples in long term relationships, where there was a tacit agreement that if sex resulted in a pregnancy, then the man would willingly do the right thing and marry his partner in haste.

Pregnancy without marriage was a personal and social disaster for an unmarried woman where marriage was not an option for whatever reason and where traditional methods of bringing about a miscarriage had failed. Back-street abortion was illegal and dangerous in the extreme and was a solution only for the desperate. Not only was the status of an unmarried mother that of a social pariah and, without the possibility of marriage, she was left with only two realistic choices: to bring up the child on her own, hopefully with the backing of her family as little or no help was available from the state, or to give up her baby for adoption. Great pressure was often applied by official agencies on vulnerable young women to consider the latter choice, as adoption conveniently solved two of society's problems at a stroke – the financial support of an illegitimate child and the emotional needs of infertile and childless couples. Whatever a girl decided to do, the term 'unmarried mother' carried with it implications of immorality, usually unjustified, and the real threat of being rejected by friends and relatives. Immediate families often went to great lengths to conceal a pregnancy in an attempt to avoid the otherwise inevitable social repercussions. Some young women were even hidden in the home or were sent away to give birth in far-away hostels where they remained until their babies were adopted. In my late teens, two of my friends became single parents and I found it hard to accept the unkind treatment that they were forced to endure while, at the same time, their errant partners derived some measure of respect among their male contemporaries. My father said that I should not associate with women like that.

Almost every week during my time at university there was a party to attend somewhere or other, occasionally by personal invitation but, more often than not, by just turning up and gate-crashing. Sheila, Marjory, John and me held our fair share of parties, jointly in our two flats at 434 East Park Road. Sheila and Marjory's lounge was normally decorated with bunting and cleared for dancing, while our upstairs kitchen was used as a bar and our small lounge for intimate conversation. The stairs were often used as an overflow if everywhere else was full. Parties not only provided for dancing and the discussion of issues that we considered to be of great importance, they were also opportunities, or even excuses, for drinking, smoking and making new friends, usually of the opposite sex. The party hosts were expected to provide some alcoholic drink, usually in the form of a punch, an often unappetising but lethal combination of cider, cheap white wine and a spirit – brandy or rum – mixed together with slices of cucumber and a tin of fruit cocktail.

Guests brought additional alcohol for their own consumption, often bottles of wine that were sometimes added to the punch – usually cheap bottles of sweet Sauterne, Liebfraumilch, Mateus Rose or Blue Nun – or two-pint bottles of brown or pale ale. My preference was for a Party Four, a large can containing four pints of beer. Everybody smoked cigarettes so the atmosphere in every room was thick with a blue smoky haze. Any guests with a musical talent arrived carrying their instruments, keen to entertain with an impromptu jazz session, a folk song or to provide the accompaniment for communal singing. Most parties were noisy affairs and, as is often the case with young people, we showed little concern for our neighbours. I once asked our unfortunate bed-ridden house owner in her ground floor accommodation at East Park Road if our noise was a nuisance to her; she graciously responded that it was nice to hear young people enjoying themselves.

Drugs were rarely used. I had heard of 'uppers' and 'downers', Benzedrine, purple hearts, cannabis and hash but, at all the parties I ever attended during my first three

Party time at East Park Road.

years at university, I was neither offered nor aware of anyone using drugs. Undoubtedly there were some users, but the fashion for recreational drugs did not explode until later in the 1960s. Our drugs of choice were exclusively alcohol, nicotine and caffeine, and our intake of these was frequently limited by a lack of money. Yet, by 1964, the distinctive sweet smell of cannabis smoke had become more common at parties and dances although, for most of us, drug taking was still regarded as a wealthy person's addiction. I had far more important things on which to spend my limited finances.

Parties also provided a great opportunity for embarrassing blunders. In my first year at university, I was invited to a party held jointly by two tutors from the Philosophy Department for all the students attending their courses. The food was excellent but I was surprised to find that the only alcohol available was either red or white wine, which we all consumed in large quantities. The party ended abruptly around midnight when a lecturer's wife was impressively sick, fouling the kitchen and toilet with a half-digested mixture of potato mayonnaise and red wine. From that day onwards I have never been able to drink large quantities of wine without feeling ill. On another occasion, I attended a party held by a medical psychologist, a young woman who was the partner of a friend, and whose professional background was unfamiliar to me. On arriving at the party, I noticed that most of the guests were men, which was a great disappointment as I was hoping to make some new female acquaintances. In order to liven up what I considered to be a rather dull affair I donned one of the hostess' dresses and, encouraged by another male guest, I flounced into the lounge of her flat shouting 'Look out boys, here is the talent at last'. I was immediately pushed out of the lounge by the hostess herself who explained in no uncertain terms that many of the party guests were her male homosexual patients. For the rest of my time at the party, I hid myself in a corner pretending to be paralytically drunk in order to avoid the possible unwelcome attention of some of her clients. I was indeed an innocent abroad. I was aware of homosexuality and, as an unsympathetic teenager, had told jokes about it but, until that moment, I had not even considered the possibility that some of the people I knew might be gay.

Homosexuality was a topic frequently discussed at the university and one where my opinions were confused. I had been brought up in an era when homosexuality and homosexual practices were illegal and were considered by many to be symptomatic of a decline in civilised behaviour. Influenced by the prejudices of the time, I came to the inaccurate conclusion that homosexuality was associated with indecency in toilets, high-jinks at public schools and old men corrupting young boys, especially scout leaders, ballet dancers and choir masters. As a result, it involved a massive learning step for me to appreciate that it could involve a close and permanent relationship between two caring adults of the same gender. The 1957 Wolfenden Committee had recommended a relaxation of the laws for consenting adults but it was not until 1966 that this relaxation became legal. It was not surprising that the whole question of homosexuality was a hot topic in my student days. In 1960, a lively autumn session of the university's Friday night Debating Society considered the motion 'That homosexual practices between consenting adults in private should not be contrary to British law'. The motion was passed with a large majority, although I suspected at the time that not all of those who voted for the motion were either convinced by the arguments or even tolerant of homosexuality. It was the liberal thing to do. Nobody, including myself, wanted to appear behind the times and out of step with the current fashionable trends in student opinion. I voted for the motion despite many misgivings, especially about the coherence and validity of some of the arguments supporting the motion, one of which suggested that homosexuality was an abnormal mental condition and, therefore, untreatable by confinement in prison, and not that it was a natural and acceptable state for some people.

CHAPTER 9

FOREIGN AFFAIRS

The final days of the 1961 Easter Term were a sad time for me as many of my continental friends from Club 57 had completed their stay in Leicester and were returning home, including the Austrian twins – one of whom, Krista, had been my girlfriend for the previous month or more. Our fond farewells were accompanied by an invitation to visit them both at their home in Austria during the coming summer holiday, an invitation that I promised faithfully to keep. Soon after my return to Rollesby for the Easter vacation, I received a letter from them saying that before returning to Austria they had embarked on a grand tour of England and were hoping to visit me in Norfolk during the following week.

My mother was exceedingly concerned when I told her that we were about to receive visitors, especially as they were foreign visitors. Nevertheless, the house was quickly tidied, cleaned and the spare bed made up in preparation for their arrival. My father was somewhat tight-lipped about the visit as his army service during World War Two had resulted in a deep distrust of foreigners, especially Germans, Austrians, Italians and anyone from the Orient. Like most of my generation, I retained few memories of wartime and gave little thought to the errors of the past; but for my parents the horrors, sacrifices and enforced separations that war had involved were still vivid and they had great difficulty in regarding old enemies as new friends, even the innocent children of old enemies. My father was extremely conscious and resentful of the fact that he had been forcibly separated from his family for nearly seven years because of war, initially with the RAF building airfields and then on war service in Italy and Austria with the Royal Engineers. Leave was infrequent and, as a result, the important father-son bonding of early childhood did not take place between us as it should have done. Inevitably, our subsequent relationship was not as close as it might have been. When he was finally demobbed from the army in February 1947 I was six years of age, and not only did I regard him as a stranger in our house but I also greatly resented sharing my mother's affection with him. While our relationship grew stronger over time, we both still found it extremely difficult openly to demonstrate our affection for one another.

Other than my father's war service, neither of my parents had strayed much beyond the borders of Norfolk and had certainly never travelled as peacetime visitors to the continent of Europe. When the twins eventually arrived, hosts and guests got on together exceedingly well and their short stay passed without incident. Yet, it was apparent to me that our home was not quite what they expected, although they tolerated the hardships of rural Norfolk with extreme good grace. They were clearly unused to a home with neither a bathroom nor hot running water and no indoor lavatory, only an outside bucket toilet inhabited by spiders. When they finally left, my mother said that, although she thought them to be extremely nice women, she hoped that I was not contemplating a permanent involvement with a 'foreigner', especially one who normally spoke German. As I was still undecided on that matter, I declined to make any comment.

Immediately after Easter and one week before the start of the summer term, I returned to Leicester early because I was required to assist at a practical field excavation as part of my assessment for the module in British Archaeology. During the 1950s and 1960s, the Archaeology Department at Leicester University developed and assessed the practical skills of its students through their assistance on a number of rescue excavations in Leicestershire and Rutland. The assessment for my year group took place at Breedon on the Hill in Leicestershire, where an Iron Age hill fort was under threat from nearby quarrying for stone. Under the direction of Mr Thomas and Mr Dyer, archaeologists from the university, we excavated and recorded a section through the ramparts of the hill fort. It was extremely interesting, not only to see how clear the evidence was in the ground for long decayed posts and filled-in ditches, but also to join in the excitement of the professional archaeologists when small and barely recognisable pieces of pottery were found. On our final day at Breedon, we were re-directed to a flat area immediately adjacent to the quarry's edge where we excavated an Anglo-Saxon burial ground that was about to be destroyed by blasting. As we began to reveal the various skeletal remains, many of us felt some pangs of remorse as we realised that archaeology was not just about excavating buildings, castles, posts and ditches but was also about disturbing the remains of real, once-living human beings. It was with some regret that we hurriedly packed their bones into cardboard boxes in the knowledge that they were destined, eventually, to provide evidence for research into diseases of the past.

The rest of that summer term was devoted to reading and revision for the examinations in late May and early June. However, I approached the examinations with some trepidation as I had missed numerous lectures, usually as a result of oversleeping after far too many late nights spent partying with my friends. British Archaeology had been extremely interesting, but my potential as an archaeologist was limited by a lack

**My attempt to emulate Professor Mortimer Wheeler. Digging up a hill fort in
Leicestershire, April 1961.**

of historical knowledge, particularly about the Roman Empire. My past enthusiasm for
Animal, Vegetable, Mineral proved not to be the best preparation for archaeological studies
at university level. Despite the loss of Mr Harré to a lecturing post at Oxford, I
continued to perform best in the Logic and Scientific Method module.

During that summer term my flatmates John, Sheila and Marjory were all preoccupied with teaching practice in various junior schools. Unfortunately, Sheila and Marjory were placed in schools a long way from Leicester and were forced to relinquish their tenancy of the first floor flat. Seizing the opportunity, John and I replaced them on the first floor, primarily to gain possession of the bathroom, while our two-roomed attic accommodation passed into the hands of two first year university women who had become dissatisfied with their allocated lodgings. Sheila and Marjory were sadly missed. They had become the older sisters that I would have loved but never had, and had provided me with advice when needed and a shoulder to cry on in times of despair. A platonic friendship with two young women was a new and satisfying experience for me; prior to that I had assumed that all close male-female relationships were essentially sexual in nature.

Once the summer term was over, I returned to Norfolk and began working as a counter attendant at Alfredo's coffee shop in Great Yarmouth in order to raise funds for my proposed hitchhiking trip to see the twins in Austria. Alfredo's coffee shop was a small seafront snack bar owned by my Uncle Bob's brother-in-law, Alfie. Alfie was a short, middle-aged man of Italian descent, sharp in look, manner and dress, and a very astute businessman. Located at the seaside end of Regent Road, the bar was extremely busy during the summer holiday season and so, every year, Alfie employed one or two students to help with his family-run business. My summertime colleague behind the counter was Ted, a self-confident art student from Lincolnshire with a talent for charming the girls. Throughout the summer I became quite adept at making and selling all types of sandwiches and rolls, hotdogs and burgers, tea, coffee and cold drinks, ice creams, ice cream sodas, fruit sundaes, Knickerbocker Glories and banana splits, despite my previous lack of culinary skills.

Working with Ted was great fun as his risqué banter with the female customers guaranteed that the coffee bar was regularly filled with good-looking young holidaymakers. In our free time, we made full use of Great Yarmouth's holiday attractions in our search for female companionship, especially at the Botton Brother's Pleasure Beach on the southern tip of the Golden Mile. Once the shop was closed in the evening and most of Great Yarmouth's visitors had returned back to their holiday accommodation, the seafront came alive again when the many students and casual workers from the amusement arcades, hotels and restaurants gathered together to relax after a day's hard work. Late night football matches along the deserted promenade or liaisons under the pier were common occurrences but, more often than not, at weekends Ted and I joined the staff and residents of nearby hotels in their licensed bars for after-hours drinks and conversation.

Our favourite destination was the Queen's Hotel, immediately opposite to Alfredo's at the end of Regent Road, a popular hotel with many of the servicemen based at the various American airfields in East Anglia, where we bartered for American cigarettes as well as joining the hotel's student employees for drinks and the occasional game of poker. The bars at the Queen's Hotel were well stocked with jukeboxes and played current rock 'n' roll hits at full volume, including many American imports. The rooms were cleared for dancing and, from early evening, young local women and female holidaymakers sat on benches arranged along the walls hoping to attract an American companion. Fights happened with monotonous regularity, usually between the servicemen and their jealous local rivals. Working as a chambermaid at the Queen's was Diane, a fashion student from the Leicester Art and Tech, whom I promised to meet with once we were both back in Leicester for the coming autumn term.

At last, on the morning of Monday 14 August 1961, I set off for Austria on my first Continental adventure with my ex-army kitbag on my shoulder, my guitar slung over my back and my newly acquired passport, £40 in traveller's cheques and some German marks for travel expenses in my pocket. The first part of my journey passed without incident. To save money, I hitchhiked to London and then on by train to Dover, where I caught the overnight ferry to Ostend in Belgium. My intention was to hitchhike across Europe to my destination, the small town of Steyr in Austria, where I was to meet with the twins and spend a week or more in their company before hiking back home again. On a map, the route looked simple – Ostend to Steyr via Aachen, Bonn, Stuttgart, Munich, Salzburg, and Linz. As most of the route was by autobahn, it was a journey that I estimated would take me no more than two days.

However, my problems began immediately. After seizing just a few hours of sleep on the overnight ferry, I arrived in Ostend at 6.30am to discover that Tuesday 15 August 1961 was a Belgian national religious holiday, held to celebrate the Assumption of the Blessed Virgin, and all the roads were deserted. It seemed to me that I trudged along the highway out of Ostend for hours, waving my pre-prepared notice indicating my destination – Germany/Austria – at the few cars that passed me, before, at last, one stopped and an English voice called out, 'Germany? Hop in'. My saviour informed me that, despite his civilian dress, he was a soldier in the British Army returning back from leave and could take me as far as Aachen, just over the border into Germany. The journey of about 100 miles, driven at speeds in excess of 70 miles an hour, was over very quickly. My only concern was that my companion appeared not to stop at a Belgium-Germany border check-point when indicated to do so by the border officials. I can only conjecture why he did not do so but, true to his word, he eventually dropped me at a slip road on the main Aachen to Köln highway.

As it happened, my problems were still far from over because the slip road contained a dozen or more other hikers all enthusiastically waving their destination notices at the few passing cars. My neighbour on the side of the road, a young German hitchhiker, eventually enquired in perfect English where I was going and said that, as the main road appeared to be crowded, he was heading for Koblenz across country and would be happy if I were to join him. Having nothing to lose, I agreed and followed my new companion down a side road to an unknown destination. After a number of relatively short lifts through a most picturesque hilly and forested countryside, an area that he proudly explained was an important German wine producing region, we arrived late in the evening at a small village where he knew there was a German Youth Hostel, a Jugendherberge. Unfortunately, in my haste to leave England, I had failed to register as a member of the Youth Hostel Association and was not eligible to stay there. In fact, I had given little thought at all to where I might stay overnight during my journey to Austria. Luckily, my new friend acted as the perfect host to a stranger in his country, as he immediately found me bed and breakfast accommodation in a nearby farmhouse where, after a welcome supper of bread and cheese, my first food since leaving the cross-channel ferry, I collapsed into bed and slept soundly under a duvet for the very first time in my life.

The next morning after an early breakfast, my German friend collected me from the farmhouse and we set off once again on the road to Koblenz. Breakfast had been a most bizarre event as neither the farmer nor his wife spoke any English and, as I spoke no German, our conversation consisted entirely of grunts and hand gestures. Nevertheless, I was most grateful for the substantial breakfast of cold sausage, ham, bread, cheese and coffee. I eventually discovered that my companion on the road, a student from the University of Heidelberg, was a seasoned traveller and spent most of his summer holidays hiking around Europe. He was well equipped for the task, dressed in leather shorts, long socks and hiking boots, with a large haversack on his back containing everything he needed for a hiking trip. At midday we shared his lunch of water from a flask, rye bread and a large cold sausage which he cut into pieces with an impressively sharp sheath knife. I, on the other hand, was ill-prepared for hiking, dressed as I was in a donkey jacket, sweater, jeans and elastic-sided suede boots. My shoulders ached from carrying my heavy army kitbag as well as my guitar. Nevertheless, my German friend expressed his delight at finding a British student on the road. He explained that exploring the continent on foot or by bicycle was

Hitchhiking to Austria, 1961. Hiking while carrying a kitbag and guitar proved to be exhausting.

considered essential character training for German youth and that the absence of English travellers confirmed the opinion held by most continentals that young people in England were unadventurous, insular and lazy. Despite my inadequate preparation for the journey to Austria, he considered me to be a novel exception to that rule.

We eventually arrived at Koblenz late that afternoon. Koblenz, I discovered, was a historic German town located at the confluence of the Rhine and Moselle rivers, a town dominated from a high hilltop by the immense and impressive Ehrenbreitstein Fortress. However, as I was tired and just passing through on my way to Austria, sightseeing was not on my agenda. Before taking his leave, my travelling companion arranged for me to stay for the night at an impressively cheap town centre hotel. After a supper consisting of stewed steak and vegetables, with a bottle of lager beer – Hobson's choice as the only words I could recognise on the restaurant menu were 'steak' and 'bier' – I retired to bed. To my surprise, the bedroom contained three double bunk-beds and it was clear that, at worst, I would be sharing with five other residents. Luckily, there was little demand for a bed that night and I had only to share my accommodation with a Dutchman who spoke some, often unintelligible, English and a drunken Eastern European who snored.

Realising that my progress hitchhiking across Europe was far too slow, the next morning I found my way to Koblenz railway station and, after cashing some of my precious traveller's cheques, I bought a single ticket to Linz on a Vienna-bound train. My adventures continued on the railway station when I failed to realise that I should pay the female lavatory attendant to open the doors of the cubicles in the men's toilet and entered a cubicle left open by its previous occupant, only to find that the doors bolted automatically when closed and I was securely locked inside. Eventually, by yelling and banging hard on the door, I managed to attract the attendant's attention and I was let out by an irate young woman demanding money. By comparison, the rail journey from Koblenz to Linz was a pleasant and uneventful episode.

After a short rail journey from Linz, I finally arrived at Steyr early in the evening of Thursday 17 August and made my way to the address where the twins were lodging for an enthusiastic and tearful reunion. Eventually, they took me to view the holiday accommodation that they had arranged for me, which turned out to be a large two-roomed wooden garden shed located on a vegetable allotment belonging to a swarthy middle-aged man who, on all the occasions that I met him, was dressed in what appeared to be a well-worn ex-World War Two German army uniform. The shed, equipped with electricity and a cold water tap, was furnished with a single bed, a table, two chairs and numerous garden tools in one of the rooms, and a sink, washing machine and spin dryer in the other. Despite being very basic, it was sufficient for my needs and had been extremely cheap to hire.

I was then taken to a cellar bar where I met some of Krista and Karin's Austrian friends, most of whom spoke excellent English. On a number of occasions during the evening, I noticed that two or more of the male members from our party disappeared and returned with a third stranger who then offered to buy me a beer. When I asked Krista why this was happening she explained that, knowing where I came from, some of the rougher elements in the bar were objecting to my presence and making insults about England and the English. Her friends were merely persuading them that I was indeed a welcome guest. When I suggested that I was quite able to defend the honour of the English myself, she suggested that it would be better for all of us if I just drank the beer.

In the morning, I was collected from my garden shed by Horst, to whom I had been introduced the previous evening and who had clearly been allocated the task of looking after me while Krista was working during the day. Horst, a student in his early 20s, spoke perfect English and proved to be an excellent daytime companion. Under his guidance, we conducted an intensive exploration of the facilities of Steyr, an exploration which consisted mainly of talking, smoking, eating sausages of many shapes and sizes, and drinking beer and coffee in numerous restaurants and bars.

In the evening, I was introduced to Krista and Karin's parents, who had travelled especially from Linz to Steyr, undoubtedly with the prime intention of inspecting their daughters' foreign visitor. It was a meeting that proved to be difficult because neither of their parents spoke much English. Their father was a most confident and pleasant man who, I quickly gathered, was an eminent high court judge and a man of some importance in the district. I can only guess what he thought when he met a rather dishevelled young Englishman dressed in jeans, a donkey jacket and elastic-sided boots. Nevertheless, at the end of the evening, he informed me that a friend had given him the use of a large residence at Innsbruck in the Austrian Tyrol and that he was taking his family, including the twins, there on Sunday for a two day break and would be delighted if I would join them. Naturally, I agreed, not just to be with my friends, but to experience the Alpine scenery. I had expected to be surrounded by mountains in Austria and was most disappointed to discover that the area around Linz and Steyr was quite flat, not unlike parts of Leicestershire and Norfolk.

On the Saturday evening I was invited to a small party at Horst's flat, where I was introduced to the local drink, schnapps; a clear innocuous looking alcoholic fluid with a kick like a mule. At one point in the evening I was persuaded to join a line of young men who were all apparently holding a large tumbler full of schnapps. I too was provided with a similar tumbler. I was then informed that most Austrian men of any quality could drink a tumbler full of schnapps at one go, after which, one by one, they all drained their glasses. Being foolhardy, I immediately said that whatever an Austrian could do an Englishman could do as well, and proceeded quickly to swallow my schnapps. The kick was immense and for minutes I could hardly breathe. Krista was furious; 'They only had water', she admitted. As Austrian honour was now at stake, Horst poured himself a large tumbler full of schnapps which he then drank with a similar breathless outcome. Although we were both unscathed by the experience, the twins insisted on plying Horst and me with numerous glasses of water and slices of brown bread covered thickly with salt, with the eventual inevitable outcome. The following morning, before setting out for Innsbruck, I had coffee with a hung-over Horst and I confessed to him that, although I was enjoying my stay in Austria, the spark appeared to be missing from my relationship with Krista. Horst clearly understood the situation as he pointedly remarked, 'You may be a King in your country, but here you are just a stranger who is finding it hard to fit in'.

The stay in Innsbruck was a great delight and I was entertained extremely well by Krista's family. The Tyrolean mountain scenery was beautiful and a magnificent contrast to the dull countryside around Steyr. The highlight of my stay was a trip on a cable car to the 7,657ft summit of Hafelekar Peak, a mountain just outside of Innsbruck. Back in Steyr, as things had not developed positively on the personal front, I decided that it was time for me to return home. Horst and the twins organised a farewell party for me at the allotment where, after much beer and schnapps, things deteriorated when one of the guests decided to set fire to my bedding, which was then quenched with a bucket of water and the pail thrown through the glass window of the shed. After many apologies, at least from some of Krista's friends, the party dispersed and I was left to clear up the resulting mess as best I could. Tactfully, I left the twins to explain the reason for the devastation to the shed's owner.

The next morning, I bade a sad farewell to Krista and Karin and made my way by train to Linz. My Austrian hosts had been so generous that I discovered I had enough money left to travel back to England by rail. Any disappointments I felt regarding the outcome of my trip were alleviated somewhat by the truly memorable return train journey through the superb mountain scenery of the Austrian and Swiss Alps. After travelling through the night, the train arrived at Calais, where I caught the ferry back to England. When I eventually returned to my home in Norfolk, my parents sympathised but breathed a sigh of relief when I told them of my adventures and of the disappointing but not unexpected outcome to my visit. There were certainly too many differences in language, culture and class, and too many people at home and abroad with long-held prejudices conspiring against us for any permanent relationship to develop between me and my Austrian girlfriend.

CHAPTER 10

DISCOVERING THE HARDSHIPS OF LIFE

One week before the start of the following autumn term, I returned to Leicester in order to find accommodation for the new academic year. Having successfully qualified as a teacher, John had left 434 East Park Road in July and so I was forced to relinquish the tenancy as I could not afford to continue renting our flat for the summer vacation on my own. Nevertheless, as soon as I arrived back in Leicester I returned to 434 East Park Road, not just to arrange for the collection of the trunk that I had stored for the summer in an outside shed, but also in the hope that one of the flats was still unoccupied. Unfortunately both were taken but, having nowhere else to go, I managed to persuade the new student tenants of the top flat to allow me to sleep on the kitchen floor while I arranged alternative accommodation for myself. After a most uncomfortable night spent sleeping fitfully on the hard and cold linoleum-covered surface, I made my way into the university, where I joined a dozen or more other students in the JCR at the Percy Gee searching through the advertisements in the *Leicester Mercury* for flats to rent. Later that morning I accompanied Mike, a third year engineering student, to view an apartment for two people that had become available at Gopsall Street, a mere half-mile walk from the university.

With the growing number of students studying not just at the university but also at Leicester's many colleges, finding accommodation was rapidly becoming a problem. The various halls of residence barely provided enough accommodation to cater for the first year intake and some second year students. Other students were forced either to accept approved lodgings or to seek accommodation on their own. In the early 1960s, very few students lived at home; it was usual for unmarried students to seek independence from their parents by studying at universities well away from their home environments. Good flats were in short supply and often far too expensive for student tenants. Students were frequently not even considered as prospective tenants for the better apartments and, even where students were welcome, landlords often applied a colour bar banning Irish, black or Asian applicants. Consequently, most student flats were located in the poorer neighbourhoods and were often damp, dirty and in a poor state of repair.

My new residence, 37 Gopsall Street, was a two-up, two-down, back-to-back terraced house in a run-down working-class district of Leicester called Highfields. The two first floor rooms and the bathroom were rented by a young married couple, while the ground floor living room was used as a bed-sitting room by a university research student and his girlfriend. The apartment that was advertised for let turned out to consist solely of the small ground floor front room of the house, which had been furnished with two single beds, a table, two chairs and a wardrobe. A small kitchen and dining area to the rear of the ground floor were shared by all the tenants, while the residents of the ground floor apartments were expected to wash in the kitchen sink and use an outside toilet for personal relief. There was no heating throughout the house, other than a one bar electric fire in each of the rooms.

Mike, my new flatmate, was a tall and hard-working engineering student also in his third year. Our paths had not crossed until then, so we had each developed our own circle of friends. Nevertheless, for the duration of our stay at Gopsall Street, we maintained a friendly coexistence, although we both continued to go our separate ways at the university. Indeed, the accommodation was so damp, cold and unappealing that we spent as little time there as possible. With the exception of those occasions when we used the premises for a party, Mike normally spent the weekends away from the flat and I used it only as a place to sleep. The great advantage of rooming with Mike was that he owned a car, a rare possession for a student in the 1960s. On cold and damp mornings it was a great pleasure to be driven in comfort to the university even though his car often needed a push to get it to start. Car-owning students were few and far between, and many, like me, did not even possess a driving licence. Neither cars nor motorcycles were permitted to first year students in hall. Nevertheless, some of the more fortunate among the student fraternity did drive cars. One flamboyant student notoriously usually arrived at the university in a vintage Rolls-Royce which he parked ostentatiously in front of the Fielding Johnston Building, while another gave lifts to his friends in a World War Two American Jeep. One fortunate student was reputed to own a 1920s Bugatti racing car. In Rollesby, hardly any of my contemporaries owned a motorcar even though many were in employment and earning a wage. A few rode motorbikes or Vespa and Lambretta scooters, the current craze among young people with spare money, but most still relied on a cycle and the bus for transportation, or simply walked.

Most of the houses along Gopsall Street were run-down, rented properties inhabited by a mix of white working-class families, many of Irish or Polish descent, and newly arrived African-Caribbean and Asian immigrants. Small corner shops supplied sweets, newspapers and some basic groceries, and a small but convenient fish and chip shop provided cheap takeaway meals. The street was part of the main red-light district

With Mike outside Gopsall Street, 1962. A student with a car was a rarity.

of Leicester and many of our female visitors were often forced to endure the unwelcome approaches of men seeking paid companionship. Generally, relationships with our neighbours were good, despite the occasional noisy party. However, compared to 37 Gopsall Street, my previous flat at 434 East Park Road was a palace.

In rural Norfolk, racial discrimination was not a pressing issue. Apart from glimpses of black and Asian crew members on the ships berthed at the docks in Great Yarmouth, or black American servicemen enjoying the recreational facilities along the seafront, my experience of people from other races was extremely limited. The holiday season apart, it was rare for me to meet with anyone originating from outside Norfolk, let alone from another country or another continent. Before university, I had direct personal contact with only three people with a racial background different to my own: a black American GI serviceman, a Chinese doctor living in Great Yarmouth and an

African teacher from Nigeria. The black GI I met briefly when I was five years old and travelling on a crowded bus back home to Rollesby from Great Yarmouth. The GI was standing in the downstairs aisle of the bus in front of my mother and me. Being a rather precocious child and fascinated by the fact that he was black, an American soldier and travelling on our bus, I pulled at his tunic and uttered the fashionable words of the time 'Got any gum, chum?' I cannot say whether there were any tensions on the bus that were caused by his presence but I can distinctly remember the smile that broke out on his face and the fact that he not only gave me a piece of his chewing gum but also gave pieces to every child sitting on the lower deck of the bus, a gesture much applauded by almost all of his fellow passengers.

The Chinese doctor, the stepfather of one of my sixth form friends, was well known in Great Yarmouth and revered for his medical skills. My aunt Doris Parnell was especially fond of the doctor as he had attended to my cousin, Deanna, after she had accidentally tipped a pan of boiling water over her face. His regular visits, expert practice and kind confident manner meant that my cousin made a full recovery devoid of any obvious scarring. In 1956, Mr Oluwole Siwoku, a teacher from Nigeria, spent some time working at Rollesby School as part of an official group engaged on a fact-finding visit to this country to study the English educational system. Mr Siwoku lodged with my grandparents at Hall Cottages for the duration of his week-long attachment to Rollesby School. When I eventually met him, Oluwole Siwoku turned out to be a short thin man with horn rimmed glasses dressed in a dark suit, grey pullover, white shirt and tie, and well-polished black shoes. For transport he had brought with him an old battered bicycle that he rode sedately, his trousers held well away from the chain by a pair of cycle clips. When he spoke, he spoke in perfect BBC English and he clearly experienced some difficulty in understanding our Broadland Norfolk dialect. His manners were impeccable and gentlemanly, and he quickly established a good personal relationship with my grandmother, who previously had been most apprehensive about his visit. Mr Siwoku was quite unlike the stereotypical version of a black African that we expected and his visit did much to dispel our misconceptions.

In Leicester things were very different. The influx of black immigrants from the West Indies and Asians from Central Africa, India and East and West Pakistan had resulted in large enclaves of African-Caribbean and Asian families settling in Leicester, mainly as tenants in rented properties in the Highfields district. It was inevitable that when I became a resident in Gopsall Street, I would meet and mix with many of my exotic neighbours. Generally, relationships between students and the new immigrant populations were good, although there were tensions between these incoming ethnic groups and the working-class white residents who considered the newcomers to be unwelcome and represented unfair competition for the few jobs available in the district. Race, apartheid and racial discrimination were constantly discussed at the university, but, other than a number of students from the Middle East, there were few foreign, black or Asian students studying at the university. So, the news that one of our lecturers was about to return from a sabbatical in America newly married to a black woman was greeted with much excitement. A mixed marriage was considered a very brave act on both their parts at a time when the United States was in the midst of much racial tension. When they finally returned, most of the male students agreed that they too would have willingly braved the wrath of right-wing America, as our lecturer's new wife was stunningly good looking.

By 1961, the Leicester Students' Union was undoubtedly becoming more and more politically minded. Students who were once called apathetic were beginning to take a more active interest in national and international politics, as well as the issues and grievances within contemporary society. The existing Conservative, Liberal, Socialist and International Societies were joined in the spring of 1962 by both a Marxist and an Anarchist Society, demonstrating a distinctly leftward, anti-authoritarian trend in student thinking at that time. The Socialist Society, with well over 100 active members, was the most influential of all these groups and found a cause to champion in the issue of racial discrimination. Although South Africa had long followed a policy of apartheid and the separate development of its different races, it was only after the 1960 Sharpeville shootings that the Students' Union finally took positive action and declared apartheid to be unacceptable and imposed a boycott on the purchase of South African goods.

Within the university, important issues were traditionally addressed, argued about and considered by informal discussion groups in the coffee bar, common room and the various halls of residence, or by listening to and judging all shades of opinion as presented in the more controlled context of the Debating Society. The Socialist, Marxist, International and Anarchist Societies, however, held hardened views that they were unlikely to be persuaded to change and inevitably began to move towards direct action instead of discussion. At the end of one long debate at which the Information Attaché from the South African Embassy was invited to speak on his government's policy of apartheid, the chairman of the International Society concluded the meeting not with the usual polite vote of thanks and an invitation for questions from the floor, but with a personal and abusive attack on their visitor, much to the embarrassment and dismay of the many less politically motivated members of the student body, like myself.

This well-publicised attack broke from tradition and certainly added to the difficulty that the Debates Committee was having in attracting potentially controversial guest speakers. Many students were also upset when the vice-chancellor banned Sir Oswald Mosley from the campus after he had been invited by the Students' Union to talk in a spring term debate concerning the issue of nuclear disarmament. Although few students supported Mosley's right-wing position or were in favour of his extremist views, the move was seen both as meddling in the affairs of the Students' Union by the university's ruling body and as an unnecessary restriction on students' ability to listen to controversial viewpoints, even if only to reject them.

Nevertheless, the fact that some students had been denied accommodation and access to leisure facilities because they were black had shocked many at the university, and it was not a total surprise when groups of students joined the picket lines outside those public houses in Leicester that had declared their premises to be for 'whites only'. While I was sympathetic to the students' cause, I did not become directly involved because I disliked confrontational methods and there was always the possibility that they could end in violence. Leicester students had definitely found their political voice, but the message and manner in which it was delivered was not always appreciated by the outside community. Although that voice belonged to a vocal minority, mainly drawn from the political left, it was a strong voice that dragged most of the student body along with it. Many on the extreme left saw student action as a means by which they could bring about social and political change. Consequently, it was soon apparent that those of more moderate opinions who wished to distance themselves from the extremist views of the left had begun to absence themselves more and more from the campus. On a lighter side, not everything at Leicester was political; in 1964 a team from Leicester University won the first televised *University Challenge* competition.

An address to new students

On behalf of the previous years at the university, I wish to welcome you to Leicester and to apologise for the uncomfortable buses, lack of good restaurants, indifferent shops and the offensive missives of the lunatic fringe who abuse the University and its students by inane polemics in the evening papers. To this list of failings must be added apologies for the dancing schools and coffee bars that don't admit coloured students, the city organisations who interfere with the Debates Committee, the lack of library facilities, theatres and decent pubs.

President's column, Ripple, 13 October 1961

What kind of university culture is this?

As one who has been very proud that there is a university in Leicester, I am greatly perturbed at the trend of recent events: (1) The publicity or notoriety of one of its professors in the defence of *Lady Chatterley's Lover*, (2) The defence of the 'Sherry Tea-Time' at the opening of the new College Hall and since then, for fear students might not be tempted to have their first drink, the subtle provision of a menu containing home-cured ham braised in cider and wine known as Leicester University Hunting Port, (3) The invitation to Sir Oswald Moseley to the proposed Nuclear Armament debate.

I have been through three wars and vividly remember the Fascist antics of Sir Oswald and his Blackshirts and am beginning to wonder what culture and reputation Leicester University is trying to build for itself. How many thoughtful parents will feel they can send their young people to where it is evident an atmosphere is being created which is unhelpful to the moral and social character of those who would deserve to become not only learned but trustworthy leaders of the future.

Correspondence, *Leicester Mercury*, 22 February 1961

For my final year as an undergraduate, I registered for the third year course in Pure Mathematics and elected to study History of Science as my subsidiary module. After some persuasion, I was also proposed as a candidate in the elections for various posts of responsibility within the Students' Union and was rewarded with a position on the RAG Committee where I became the editor of the RAG Magazine, *Lucifer*, as well being appointed as booking secretary for the Leicester University Film Society.

For most of my time at university, money and 'making ends meet' were perpetual problems. After my A level success and the reward of a place at university, I had been awarded a Norfolk Major Scholarship, which meant that the Norfolk Education Committee paid all my tuition and examination fees at Leicester University. As my father was a low wage earner, it also entitled me to a maintenance grant for my daily living expenses of £280 per annum. Without this scholarship I would not have been able to undertake three years of study at a university. My father could not afford to pay my fees or help greatly with my daily expenditure, and student loans did not exist – not that a loan would have been acceptable. The idea of borrowing money or having a debt was alien to both my parents. The most regularly quoted of all the mottos that guided their daily lives were: 'Never a borrower or lender be' and 'What you can't afford you can't have'. When I was still at school and dependent financially upon my father, he naturally regarded himself as being responsible for any decisions about my day to day expenses and he would never have allowed me to incur a debt. My parents even considered the growing popularity for buying goods on the 'never-never' a travesty and were horrified when, in 1964, I bought bedroom furniture on a hire-purchase agreement. With my maintenance grant of £280 together with potential earnings from holiday work, they considered that I should, from that time forward, be able to look after myself financially and perhaps make some contribution, however small, towards the household budget when I returned home during university vacations. In their opinion, they had already supported me for an extra three years at school and their duty of support was now ended. It was abundantly clear to me that it was essential for me to find regular employment during university vacations.

Holiday work was plentiful in Norfolk, especially during the summer months. Students were in great demand as casual labourers in agriculture at harvest times and as general workers at Norfolk's coastal resorts during the peak holiday period of July, August and early September. As well as summer employments at Caister Holiday Camp, the Great Yarmouth Birds Eye factory during the pea harvest and Alfredo's coffee bar, in the winter breaks I worked on the Christmas post, delivering and sorting mail. Like most students, I spent most of my Easter vacations revising for the summer term examinations. Only once (two weeks before the end of the autumn term during my time at East Park Road) did I run out of money and ask for assistance from my parents. Their response to my request was to send me a postal order for 2s 6d, a box of apples and a long letter demanding that I should learn to manage my finances more efficiently in the future.

Officially, the university discouraged students from working during the vacations. Maintenance grants, together with parental contributions, were considered to be sufficient to cover expenses not only in term time but also during the time spent away from university, and students were expected to use their holidays for study and not as an opportunity for increasing their income. Students intending to undertake holiday work were required by the university to seek permission from their Dean of Faculty. However, most students worked during their vacations and I cannot recollect that any of them ever sought their Dean's permission. I would have not been able to exist for the whole year on my grant alone and I never considered seeking permission to work.

Luckily, my grant from the Norfolk Education Authority was always paid well before the start of each term. Some students had to wait weeks before their Education Authorities released any maintenance money. The only difficulty for me was that my grant was paid termly by cheque and so I needed to open a bank account. At the time, my parents had no need to use a bank. My father's wages were paid weekly in cash and were used to cover our weekly household expenditure. Like many working-class men, every Friday my father handed his unopened wage-packet to my mother, who then removed all the money she needed for running the household and returned what was left to him as pocket-money. The money needed to pay monthly bills she put aside into a collection of tins which she kept in a drawer. Their savings consisted solely of a small emergency fund that mother had deposited in a Post Office account. We did not take holidays away from home because my father used his two weeks statutory holiday to cover days of bad weather in the winter when otherwise he would have been laid off from work with no pay.

My girlfriend for most of my stay at Gopsall Street was Diane, my previous summertime acquaintance from the Queen's Hotel in Great Yarmouth, whom I had met again, by chance, at a Friday-night jazz session in the university's Cellar Club. Diane was a short attractive blonde with a Bridget Bardot style appeal who quickly became popular with all of my friends. All too frequently, Diane had to patiently sit and wait while I played my guitar in a rock 'n' roll band or at meetings of the university's Folk Song Society. We enjoyed a full and hectic social life together, which regularly used up most of my spare capital. Entertainment was frequently financed at the expense of food. However, there was little point in shopping for food to cook at 37 Gopsall Street as the catering facilities were extremely basic and the kitchen cupboards were infested with mice. Mike and I usually ate at the university or at a local café, and sometimes we had a takeaway meal from the fish and chip shop, but when money was tight I would often eat cold baked beans with a spoon straight from the tin. On one occasion I discovered some small inexpensive tins on the shelves at Boots' chemist shop in the centre of Leicester, which I assumed to be individual portions of food, and selected a tin of prunes and semolina for a teatime treat. Back at Gopsall Street, I discovered that the tin contained pre-prepared baby food and not, as I naively thought, a small portion for an adult. Nevertheless, I enjoyed the treat just the same. Another time, Diane brought around some eggs for our meal but the only other item in the kitchen cupboard to accompany the eggs was an ancient packet of sage and onion stuffing. Showing some initiative with a frying pan, Diane invented a new dish that we christened 'Stuffing Pancakes'.

The only time that good food was served at Gopsall Street was when Mike described our situation to a group of female students from the Domestic Science College and challenged them to serve up a wholesome Sunday meal using our facilities and our limited budgets. The challenge was accepted and four domestic science students duly arrived at Gopsall Street early one Sunday morning, complete with bags containing cooking implements and various ingredients for lunch. In no time at all, our kitchen and cooker were thoroughly cleaned, the ingredients prepared and, probably for the first time, the sounds and smells of cooking permeated the ground floor while our resident research student, his fiancée, Mike and I set out our dining table to accommodate Sunday lunch for eight. For the cost of a basic one course meal at our local café, our four Domestic Science College friends prepared for us all a substantial three course lunch of melon slices as a starter, followed by a main course of meat stew, potatoes and vegetables, and finished off with a pudding of apple crumble and custard. Never was a Sunday lunch enjoyed more.

CHAPTER 11

AZTEC, THE INCAS AND AN ORIGINAL ROCK MUSICAL

Although I had a continuing interest in playing folk music and a secret passion for rock 'n' roll, for most of my second year at Leicester my musical focus was jazz. Through my friendship with John at East Park Road, jazz dominated my musical development. From 9 to 15 March 1961, Leicester University was host to a group of 30 young people from Russia, a small but not insignificant gesture aimed at developing friendship and understanding between students from two different cultures precariously close to war. Their visit happened to coincide with the 1961 RAG Week, which certainly provided the Russians with a misleading view of student life in Britain. I first met our Russian visitors on the evening of Thursday 9 March, when they were given the best seats available for the midnight performance of the 1961 RAG Revue. From the dour expressions on their faces it was patently obvious that they were not only exhausted by their journey from Russia, but also totally confused by the revue-style entertainment on stage – an experience that can have done little to convince this presumably hand-picked group of young men and women that western culture was on a par with that in the east. My sole but noisy and un-musical contribution to the 1961 revue was as a car horn player in the pit orchestra.

Their confusion was undoubtedly exacerbated by the fact that the audience for the midnight show had been restricted to students only and, consequently, the revue contained far more explicitly vulgar material than was allowed in the two early evening performances that were open to the general public. Like the revue of 1960, the finale of the performance was a parody of a popular TV music show, but on this occasion the leading vocalist was my folk singing compatriot and friend, Rod Davies, now in his second year as a Zoology student, who performed in the revue under the stage-name of Rod Eldorado and was backed by a rock 'n' roll group who called themselves The Apaches, all of whom were dressed as pirates, complete with patches over one eye. As a finale, Rod delivered a smouldering version of *Mean Woman Blues*, which received screaming acclaim from many young women in the audience; a reaction that was no doubt encouraged by the substitution of new and extremely risqué lyrics to the song and his frequent and suggestive pelvic thrusts.

A rocking performance of *Mean Woman Blues* by Rod Eldorado and the Apaches during the 1961 RAG Revue.

The Leicester University Students' Union continued to play an active role in the visit of our Russian comrades by inviting them to participate in a variety of social activities. The craze of the moment was tiddlywinks and Leicester was basking in the title of British University Tiddlywinks champions. The carpet in the Junior Common Room was frequently covered by students practicing their winking skills, and so the Russians were dragged into the game and were invited to participate in a RAG day tiddlywinks tournament at the Town Hall in Leicester. After the tournament, the university Folk Song Society regaled the visitors with an evening performance of folk songs in the Percy Gee coffee bar. The session was organised by Roy Bailey, a British folk song enthusiast with a bushy black beard, who normally sang traditional ballads and sea shanties unaccompanied with one finger in his ear. As usual, Dave Cousins and I were among the performers and, to begin with, the session was a great success. Roy began the proceedings in a typically enthusiastic manner by standing on a coffee table and singing unaccompanied a raucous version of *Oh, Mrs MacGraw the Sergeant Said*. When it was their turn to sing, the Russians delivered an impressive rendition of the ever popular *Midnight in Moscow*. Most of the members of the university's rugby club were also present in the coffee bar, indulging in their traditional Saturday post-match drinking session, and so, inevitably, they hijacked the event and treated the Russians to rowdy versions of *Ivan Scavinsky Scavar*, *The Wild West Show* and *The Engineer's Song*.

Fortunately, the visitors failed to comprehend the obscene lyrics to these songs, as they clapped enthusiastically and presented us all with badges celebrating Russian space achievements. My badges adorned the lapels of my corduroy jacket for the rest of my time at university.

The Russian student visitors said 'niet'

Yesterday evening the visitors attended a rock 'n' roll and jazz dance held at the Corn Exchange as part of the Rag programme. It was their first experience of this type of music. Although at first they watched the 800 unconventionally dressed students letting themselves go with serious and baffled interest, towards the end of the evening they were on the floor themselves dancing their own versions to the music.

Leicester Mercury, 11 March 1961

At the start of the following autumn term I was informed by Rod that, because his performance as the singer Rod Eldorado in the spring term RAG review had been so successful, he was trying to form a rock 'n' roll band with a group of second year students. The performers he had already recruited were currently practicing most evenings in the university's jazz cellar. Being a closet rock 'n' roll fan and one who had immensely enjoyed the earlier experience of *Crumbeat*, I was determined to become involved in some way. When I finally managed to track them down I discovered that the band had recently lost their bass player. Rod, now the incumbent chairman of the university's Folk Song Society, was installed as the singer, two second year Mathematicians, Trevor Smith and Russ Dear were the lead and rhythm guitarists, and Eric Flitney, another Zoologist, was the drummer. Although I had no previous experience, I managed to convince everyone that my folk club expertise with rhythm and blues music would enable me to perform effectively as a replacement on bass guitar, and so, after a brief deliberation, I became a bass guitarist and Leicester University's first rock 'n' roll band was formed.

During most of our initial practice sessions we were preoccupied with the apparently important task of selecting a name for the group. As we were not yet entirely sure if we were a serious band a few joke names were suggested, including PG Tips and the Tea Leaves and Big Foot and the Yetis, but eventually we considered numerous variations of Rod's RAG Revue stage name and finally elected to call ourselves Aztec and the Incas. It was an established tradition during the 1950s and 1960s that individual members of a popular music group always dressed alike, so we also deliberated about a uniform for the band. The relatively cheap solution that we adopted was for everyone, except Rod, to wear the same style of sweater – a furry black, grey and blue mohair garment that looked reasonably smart but caused everyone to perspire profusely during performances. More often than not, Rod performed in front of the group dressed in a sports jacket, corduroy trousers, suede shoes and a tie.

Like most universities and colleges at that time, the jazz, folk and dance band music so beloved of university students was very slowly beginning to give way to the previously less socially acceptable sound of rock 'n' roll. Contemporary with the formation of the Incas, another group was established at the Leicester Art and Tech playing under the name of James King and the Farinas, and together the Incas and the Farinas provided the rock 'n' roll entertainment at most of Leicester's many college dances and balls for the next two years. Despite the fact that most university and college students came from predominantly conservative middle-class backgrounds and favoured listening to jazz, by 1961 rock 'n' roll groups had been established in many Further Education institutions, some of whom eventually became highly successful in the popular music scene as, for instance, the Beatles, the Kinks and the Rolling Stones with their Art School backgrounds. While the imported American rock 'n' roll culture of the mid-1950s was adopted primarily by British working-class teenagers, the mid-1960s British based resurgence of rock 'n' roll appeared to be strongly influenced by student musicians who spawned innovative regional musical styles such as the 'Merseybeat' from Liverpool and a British form of Rhythm and Blues in London. Unlike the Incas, the Farinas survived and in 1966 merged with another Leicester-based band to form the nationally successful group Family, headed by the gruff-voiced singer Roger Chapman.

Despite our very different social and musical backgrounds, the Incas quickly gelled into a competent rock 'n' roll band. Rod was a very good singer and, in his Aztec persona, an excellent front man for the group. With his rugged good looks, jet black hair and the permanent hint of a five o'clock shadow, he quickly established a loyal following of female groupies. Trevor and Russ were competent musicians and song writers, and had some previous experience of playing rock 'n' roll although their musical backgrounds lay predominantly in skiffle, jazz and dance band music. Eric, a drummer with the university's jazz band, was the most inexperienced of the group where rock 'n' roll music was concerned, although he made up for this with his enthusiasm and a great sense of rhythm. Initially we played cover versions of many current hit records, predominantly those recorded by Cliff Richard and the Shadows, including *Move It*, *The Young Ones*, *Bachelor Boy* and *Apache*. My personal favourites were

The Leicester University Jazz Band (Keith Feinson, Norman Edwards, Trevor Castle, Eric Flitney and Colin Coles) prepare to take part in the semi-final of the Inter-Universities Jazz Competition, February 1962. (Leicester Mercury Media Group)

our versions of *Shakin' All Over*, originally by Johnny Kidd & the Pirates, Little Richard's hit song, *Rip it Up* and an interesting upbeat adaptation of the traditional folk song *What shall we do with the Drunken Sailor*. We even played a tongue-in-cheek rocked-up version of *How Much is that Doggie in the Window*. Our jazz backgrounds became apparent in upbeat versions of *My Blue Heaven* and *Blue Moon*, as well as in the fact that half the group had beards, a novel feature for a rock band, even in those early days. In truth, we looked more like a jazz band than a rock 'n' roll group.

The sixth member of the group was John 'Ginger' Martin, a versatile and enthusiastic technician who looked after and maintained the band's equipment. To begin with we all had our own guitars but no amplifiers, but Ginger was extremely adept at removing and utilising the Queen's Hall's microphones and loudspeaker system to provide amplification for Rod's singing and our guitar playing, even though the equipment was occasionally temperamental and prone to break down. Trevor had a red Burns Vibra electric guitar which he had borrowed from a fellow student, Bruce Grocott (later Lord Grocott, Labour Whip in the House of Lords), and Russ an amplified acoustic Hofner Congress. Occasionally, when his guitar was unavailable, Trevor played rock accompaniments on the Queen's Hall grand piano in a style reminiscent of Jerry Lee Lewis. Unfortunately, I had insufficient capital at the time to purchase an electrified bass guitar, so I was forced to play the bass part on my acoustic six-string folk guitar which had been amplified through temporary pickups attached underneath the strings.

An invitation to our first performance.

Hear this you cats. A great Rock 'n Roll Session is to be held in the Union lecture room, On Wednesday 7-30 till 10-30 with the fabulous AZTEC and the INCAS dont miss this rave, it'll be great

ADMISSION 1/-

Trevor, Rod and Russ performing at the party where Aztec and the Incas were launched on an unsuspecting student audience, October 1961.

Our first public performance was at a party that took place in a small function room to the rear of the Percy Gee, a party that we had organised to launch the group within the university. Posters and handbills advertising the event were placed in the coffee bar and on various notice boards inviting anyone to attend who might be interested in listening to live rock 'n' roll music. To our surprise, the room was crowded and it soon became clear from the encouragement that we received from our student audience that Leicester University was ready for a rock 'n' roll band. From then on, Aztec and the Incas were in great demand and we were invited to perform at student parties, during the interval at numerous Saturday hops and as one of the musical acts at the university's 1961 Christmas Ball, where we played in a crowded JCR, allegedly as a novel alternative to the main bands who were performing in the Queen's Hall and the Refectory.

Despite the growing popularity of the Incas, not everyone was

Rod, me and Russ behind, October 1961. A lack of spare capital forced me to play a bass accompaniment on my amplified folk guitar.

enthusiastic about our brand of music. Many students preferred listening to classical music rather than beat music – jazz, skiffle and rock 'n' roll. For those who enjoyed classical music, evening and lunchtime concerts were regularly held in the Queen's Hall, often involving student musicians and ensembles, and regular professional performances were held in the nearby De Montfort Hall. Before university, my personal knowledge of classical music was extremely limited. Despite music lessons every week at grammar school, in which *Peter and the Wolf* featured on more occasions than I care to recall, I had had little opportunity to become acquainted with the classical repertoire. Pupils who were not already familiar with some of the classics or able to sing in the school choir were abandoned and ignored rather than educated. At home, my parents preferred big band music and we listened mostly to the Home and Light programmes on the radio, never to the Third, and when I was alone, I listened intently to Radio Luxembourg. When my village friend Tony began listening to classical music records, we thought that he had become strange and treated him accordingly.

Before university, my first and only experience of a classical music performance was the occasion on which the senior boys of Great Yarmouth Grammar School were invited to join the audience at a lunchtime concert played by the BBC Concert Orchestra that was to be broadcast live from Great Yarmouth's Town Hall. Along with a hundred or more senior pupils, my school friend Tim and I sat uncomfortably on the hard Town Hall chairs, sweltering in the mid-day heat, listening in awe to the wall of sound emanating from the 20 or more musicians on the stage. As instructed by our tutors, Tim and I applauded enthusiastically when the music stopped, only to discover that we were the only ones showing such appreciation. Our ignorance of the piece being played was clear for all to see because we were totally unaware that a pause existed in between the piece's two movements. Not only was our ignorance patently obvious to the headmaster, with the inevitable repercussions, but also to the thousands of people listening to the concert on the radio. The conductor was clearly not amused, although many members of the orchestra smiled.

At Leicester I bought a number of classical music recordings in an attempt to rectify my ignorance, including Holst's *Planet Suite* and Beethoven's *Pastoral Symphony*, but I was unused to listening to such music. I was familiar only with the five minute sound-bites of popular music and jazz, and not with lengthy classical compositions. I was also conditioned to regard music as something to be played, sung or danced to and not just for listening to. But even so, I greatly enjoyed the stirring music of Elgar and Wagner, although I was never able to remember the titles of the pieces that I liked. Many members of the university were quite disdainful of students, like me, who had little knowledge of classical music; to them, the Incas and our music were clearly 'beyond the pale'. A preference for classical music was considered by some students to be an essential characteristic of the intellectual elite; those who preferred anything else were often branded as peasants. Despite such views, all forms of popular music were clearly gaining more followers, much to the chagrin of the traditionalists.

Why no students?

In spite of an attractively popular programme, students of the University were conspicuous by their absence from a Symphony Concert, given by the County Symphony Orchestra, held in the Queens Hall on Friday November 9. No doubt the Jazz Nite and the musical offerings in the bar played their part, and indeed, if the enjoyment of the participants is one of the hallmarks of a good performance, then the latter was the best value of the evening.

Ripple, 3 December, 1962

Despite Ginger's best efforts on behalf of the Incas, inadequate equipment remained a problem for the group until Eric spotted a possible solution to our difficulties. Every year, the Students' Union provided a grant to any theatrical group or society within the university that was willing to produce and perform either a play or a musical on stage at the Queen's Hall in the Percy Gee. To our knowledge, no theatrical group had yet made an application for the current year's grant. Seizing the initiative, Eric approached a personal friend, Keith Miller, a student of English with an interest in drama, and asked if he would consider writing a modern rock opera tailored to the skills of the group, so that we could stage it as the year's musical production. As soon as Keith agreed, we submitted a successful application for the grant under the guise of 'The Leicester University Musicals and Operatic Society'. The award of a substantial grant not only provided the money necessary to mount a rock opera, it also enabled Ginger to improve our electronic equipment, including the purchase of an extremely useful echo-chamber. For the next few months, our lives were dominated by the planning, preparation and rehearsals for the musical, entitled *A Million Miles to the Moon*, plus performances by the Incas at various society parties, the Saturday Hop and other dances, with the result that our study time was non-existent.

It was clear that if we were to be taken seriously as a rock 'n' roll group, our equipment had to improve, especially in time for the forthcoming musical production. So as soon as my spring term maintenance cheque was cleared by the bank, I went straight to Bradley's on London Road where I bought a brand new bass guitar in a

In January 1962, I used a large proportion of my Spring Term's grant to buy a bass guitar.

bright turquoise colour for the sum of £35. I also acquired a redundant second-hand homemade amplifier and a set of speakers for a further £10 from Tim Kirchin, the bass guitarist of the Farinas. By equipping myself in this way I had recklessly spent nearly half my maintenance allowance for the term which, without a financial return from our performances, would eventually leave me short of money for food and entertainment.

But at the beginning of term such considerations hardly entered my head. Russ had also invested in a solid red electric guitar and a small amplifier.

Expresso Bingo

It is rumoured within the confines of the Musical Productions Committee that at last new, fresh ideas have come to light: an original musical is being prepared by some members of the rock group. It is a remarkable change from the previous two years when we were served with the half-baked happiness on a plate that comprises 'The Student Prince' and 'The Vagabond King'. What the story will be is not yet quite clear, but it seems that it will be a variation on the 'little boy – big star' theme

Ripple, 15 December 1961

While practicing with my new bass guitar, I unwittingly made my one contribution to the musical repertoire of the group. Before the start of every rehearsal, it was my habit to test my amplification equipment by slowly playing my way up a musical scale, increasing the volume as I progressed note by note. Before long the other members of the band began to join in with me, and this habit was adopted as our signature tune, which we christened *The Inca War Dance,* and was used at every performance of the musical as a signal to our audience that the show was about to begin; it was subsequently adopted as the opening number at the start of all our engagements. At the Saturday Hop, the sound of *The Inca War Dance* was the signal for couples to return from the bars and crowd onto the Queen's Hall dance floor, ready and eager to rock 'n' roll.

For almost the whole of January and February, I was absent from many of my

FEBRUARY 22nd, 23rd and 24th

Leicester University Musicals and Operatic Society

present

AN ORIGINAL ROCK MUSICAL

Script *mainly by* KEITH MILLER

Music *mostly by* RUSS DEAR

Story *expanded by* ROD DAVIES

From *an idea by* ERIC FLITNEY

A
M
I
L
L
I
O
N
M
I
L
E
S
T
O
T
H
E
M
O
O
N

An Original Rock Musical.

118

lectures and my study was put on hold as I joined the Incas and the rest of the cast to prepare and rehearse for the three evening performances of our rock musical, *A Million Miles to the Moon*, a production that was finally staged in the Queen's Hall from Wednesday 22 to Friday 24 February 1962. Written and produced by Keith Miller, ably assisted by Eric and Rod, the story followed a popular theme of the time – working-class boy achieves fame as a pop singer, gets too big for his boots and is finally brought down to earth. The novel tear-jerking twist at the end of our story was that Jim, the singer – played by Rod, the only member of the Incas with any previous acting experience – became seriously ill and bravely soldiered on until he finally died at the height of his fame in the arms of his working-class girlfriend, Valerie, who was played delightfully by Mary Sunderland, a first year undergraduate. Jim's tragic fate brought tears to the eyes of Rod's many faithful followers.

The production of *A Million Miles to the Moon* was competent enough, but it was not without its mishaps. During one of the performances, the band's amplification equipment broke down and, in an attempt to avoid a disaster, Ginger quickly jumped onto the stage and successfully completed a repair while we all frantically ad-libbed – hopefully, nobody noticed. While the acting and the storyline were entertaining, the real achievement lay in the music. Russ and Trevor had composed nine original songs

Rehearsals for *A Million Miles to the Moon*. The ya-ya girls (Rosie Davies, Janet Thompson and Liz Horsefield) burst out laughing during a song. (R. Davies)

Because of the musical, our studies were abandoned for most of the January and February of 1962.

for the show, comparable in both music and lyrics to anything commercially available at the time – *One Track Mind*, *How Cruel*, *Love Me inYourWay*, *Your Smile*, *Shall I TellYa*, *Jeannie*, *Return*, *What Am I Living For* and *Yes I do*. The songs not only became the core of Aztec and the Inca's musical repertoire but they also received some acclaim in the Leicester press. During rehearsals, Ginger made recordings of two of the numbers, *Love Me inYourWay* and *One Track Mind*, which were subsequently cut onto a demonstration disc. Following the success of *A Million Miles to the Moon*, the Incas were in constant demand to perform at the university and other associated colleges, and occasionally at venues in the city, thus further reducing the time available for my studies.

Rock Musical at the University

A rock 'n' roll musical being staged at Leicester University is described as a musical production based on the theme 'Little Boy – Big Star' with numerous twists and side-kicks which set out to prove that, whatever the scientists say, there are A Million Miles to the Moon. Four students, Keith Miller (script), Russ Dear (music), Rod Davies (story) and Eric Flitney (ideas) are responsible for this highly entertaining show about the rise and tribulations of

Trevor, Russ and me get with it, dreaming of becoming rock stars.

a Rock 'n' roll singer. It echoes Expresso Bongo and has some catchy numbers. Some of last night's audience thought that it was some kind of Rag show, to be supported vocally by whoops and yells. It merits far more appreciative attention having a good strong story line and songs which could become popular hits.

Leicester Evening Mail, 23 February 1962

Following our musical production, a few more original songs were added to our repertoire including *The Inca Twist*. Many of these clearly expressed through their lyrics the insecurity felt by most young men of the time in their relationships with the opposite sex. But for me the lyrics were unimportant, as they were for most of my fellow rock 'n' rollers. It was the rhythm that was essential in our music, music that encouraged our audiences to dance to the beat.

Love Me in Your Way
I could go on for ever, please believe me when I say,
The worries and heartaches you bring me, wind up more and more each day.
I know you don't care for me, though you hold my hand,

I don't mind how you hurt me, you just don't understand.

As long as I can be near you, and see you a little every day,

My hopes and prayers will be answered, if you'd love me in your way.

Music and lyrics: Russ Dear & Trevor Smith

LEICESTER UNIVERSITY MUSICALS AND OPERATIC SOCIETY

presents

A MILLION MILES TO THE MOON

an original rock musical

at 8 p.m. on Thurs., 22nd and Fri., 23rd Feb. and at 2.30 p.m. on Sat., 24th Feb.

in the Percy Gee Building of the University

All tickets 3'-

bookings at the University and Lewis's, Humberstone Gate, Leicester

Willsons (Printers) Ltd., Leicester. Phone 21213.

1962 Leicester Colleges' Rag Magazine.

No sooner had the dust settled on *A Million Miles to the Moon* then I was heavily involved with the preparation for the 1962 RAG Week. As the elected editor of the RAG magazine, *Lucifer,* my time was completely taken up with the production and distribution of the magazine in time for it to be sold on RAG Day, Saturday 10 March, especially during the afternoon's carnival procession. My greatest concern was deciding on a suitable cover design for the magazine from those submitted to a competition organised by the Art School, and selecting content that would prove neither too offensive nor too crude for the tastes of the Leicestershire general public. Past experience had shown that the university's governing body were all too ready to censor what they considered to be inappropriate material. Luckily, the final product passed muster and 40,000 or more magazines were successfully circulated among the many students and organisations at the university and colleges for sale to the general public during RAG Week.

A Pale Blue Rag Mag

Rag magazines are never intended to be literate. But this year's Leicester Colleges 'Lucifer' has qualities which lift it above the usual 'rag mag'. For one thing it contains some original work that is quite amusing. Plenty of thought has gone into the bean theme. And its layout and design is generally good. Need I say it – there is the usual assortment of crisp jokes, some of them naughty but none offensive enough to make readers itch to bring out the blue pencil. The jokes weren't all that blue.

Leicester Mercury, 12 March 1962

It also happened that, during RAG Week, Cliff Richard and the Shadows were appearing at the De Montfort Hall. One evening while Aztec and the Incas were rehearsing in the jazz cellar, we were informed that guitarists Hank Marvin and Bruce Welsh from the Shadows had been spotted entering a restaurant close by the London Road Railway Station, a short distance away. Whether it was Rod or Eric I am not totally certain but somebody suggested that kidnapping Cliff Richard would be an excellent RAG Week publicity stunt. The prize for the best stunt of the week was a barrel of beer and we were sure that our idea, if successfully executed, would merit that award. How it was to be done, or where we would take him was not at all clear but we left the cellar in a state of great excitement and made our way to the restaurant where we expected to confront the rock 'n' roll star. We planned to invite Cliff to join us for coffee at my flat in Gopsall Street, where we intended to take photographs, interview him for an article in the student newspaper, *Ripple*, and then release him after about one hour. As it was for RAG, we were convinced that he would enjoy the idea and accede to our suggestion. It would also be good publicity for him as well as for RAG.

At the restaurant, we approached Hank Marvin and Bruce Welsh and asked them where we might find Cliff Richard. The two guitarists merely shrugged their shoulders and indicated that he might be dining elsewhere, possibly at a nearby Indian restaurant. Hurriedly, Eric, Rod, Russ and I made our way to the nearest Indian restaurant – the Taj-Mahal on Highfield Street – where we ordered a curry that we could barely afford, waiting for our target to arrive. After an hour it was clear that he was not going to appear so we retraced our steps, hoping to interview Hank Marvin and Bruce Welsh instead. When we eventually returned we discovered to our embarrassment that Cliff, who wore thick-rimmed glasses off stage, had been sitting on the next table to the Shadows' guitarists and we had failed to recognise him. As the joke was on us, all thoughts of proposing a publicity kidnap disappeared. Having finished his meal in peace, Cliff was more than happy to answer some questions for the newspaper article and presented us all with signed photographs. The best RAG stunt and winner of the barrel of beer was adjudged to be that executed by a group of students from the university who had kidnapped a nude model from a life drawing class at the Art and Tech. As a result, 14 students were sent down from the University for the remainder of the spring term, including a member of the Stunts Committee who had given the RAG Committee's official approval for the escapade, although he had not taken part in it himself. The model made much of her brief appearance in the headlines of the local press.

Once my duties as editor of *Lucifer* were finished, I joined the rest of the Incas on RAG Day to perform on a float in the grand carnival parade through the city's centre.

In the early 1960s, Leicester Students' RAG Day carnival procession was allegedly the longest parade of its kind in the Midlands. It was usually led by a Leicestershire colliery marching band and the RAG Queen's carriage, followed by a long procession that included many motor lorries, and horse and tractor drawn trailers holding musical bands and decorative floats based on a chosen theme. The floats were all created by the various clubs and societies from the university and Leicester's many other colleges. The procession initially gathered along University Road and, when it was complete, wound its way down the Welford Road, along Oxford Street to the High Street and on to the city centre. At the Clock Tower the procession turned into Gallowtree Gate, and continued up Granby Street and London Road to end the tour of Leicester at Victoria Park Road, where it dispersed.

Our two-tiered construction, built on the top of a long flat-back trailer, took the form of a ship with the Incas playing music from the topmost deck. Our tall construction was immediately in trouble because the mast was in danger of becoming entangled with overhead telephone and power lines and had to be hurriedly dismantled. The band that day consisted of Rod, Trevor, Russ and I, with an absent Eric replaced on drums by the energetic and larger-than-life 'Big' Tom from the Scraptoft Teacher Training College. It was not clear whether it was Big Tom's frenetic drumming or the loss of the mast that was the reason for the pronounced list developed by the ship, which soon showed signs of imminent collapse. To make matters worse, as we rounded the Clock Tower into Gallowtree Gate, a well-aimed over-ripe tomato landed smack on Rod's chest just as he was performing his version of Cliff Richard's song *The Young Ones*. It was abundantly clear that student RAG activities, Rod's singing and rock 'n' roll was not appreciated by everyone in Leicester. Soon afterwards, we all rapidly made our way down to the lower deck, not just to prevent a total collapse of the structure, but also to avoid the unrelenting shower of missiles.

Rag Street Collection a Record £3,705

A new record was set for Street Collections in the Leicester Students' Rag on Saturday – £3,705 3s 10½d. Last year's total was £3,302. Rag Organiser, Ian Partington, said 'Police have told us that the crowds which came to see the procession were the biggest ever known in the city.' Only one incident occurred. This was when a group of youths in Gallowtree Gate pelted students on one or two floats with eggs and custard pies. The students did not retaliate. First prize for the best float went to Stoughton Hall (a University hall of residence) for a reconstruction of a Mississippi river boat. Old Mother

Gallowtree Gate, Leicester; the scene of Rod's confrontation with a well-aimed tomato.

> Hubbard's Shoes gained second prize, and College Hall won third prize for its playing cards tableau. When the procession reached University Road, a cardboard Spanish Galleon made by Villiers Hall students and called 'Mispaniola' disintegrated. The entire structure fell apart but as all the floats were about to be broken up anyway it hardly mattered at all.
>
> *Leicester Evening Mail*, 12 March 1962

Sadly, by that summer the Incas were also at a turning point. The impossible dream that we all had, but dared not mention – that we would be discovered by an influential impresario and launched on the general public as a successful rock 'n' roll band – had failed to materialise. After the rock opera there had been some interest in the demonstration disc and various enquiries were received regarding the original songs from promoters allegedly involved in the music business, but these had been rejected by Trevor and Russ because they were not totally clear regarding musical copyright and the ownership of their songs. By that time, it seemed obvious to us all that we were not destined to become rock 'n' roll stars, so the decision was made to disband the group. Rod and I were about to take our final examinations and our futures had yet to be decided. Trevor, Russ and Eric were about to begin the final year of their courses and, although Russ was keen to continue with the band, the others wanted to devote more time to their studies. Undoubtedly, the difficulties that Rod and I were having in catching up with our work, Rod with zoology and me with mathematics, had influenced their decisions. And so began what turned out to be not one but a whole series of final performances that ended with the Summer Ball where, after a 30-minute delay owing to one of our regular equipment failures, we performed to an impatient and rowdy audience that included the members of Kenny Ball's Jazz Band.

Chapter 12

Responsibilities

Towards the end of my third year at Leicester, most of my time was devoted to study in a frantic attempt to make up for the many lectures that I had missed as a result of my involvement with Aztec and the Incas. The History of Science module had been so extremely interesting that, with my tutor's backing, I applied to remain at the university for two more years to study for a Master's degree in History of Science, subject to passing my final examinations at a good honours level. Despite some spelling errors, a long-standing problem I had still to overcome, my tutor indicated that the special study I had submitted as part of my assessment had achieved the necessary standard and that my future was now dependent upon my examination results. As a result of my involvement with the Incas, I struggled to complete my revision. Time was short, so I adopted the strategy of concentrating on specific topics rather than trying to cover the whole of the syllabus in detail, trusting to luck that the examination questions would match my selection.

On a personal level, things were not going too well either. I had suffered from one chesty cough after another for most of the winter, undoubtedly as a result of the damp and cold accommodation at Gopsall Street, and, because my health was not improving, I was obliged to seek help from the university doctor. When I was weighed at the surgery I was horrified to discover that my weight had dropped to almost 10 stone. The doctor's advice, offered in the severest of tones, was to eat more, get more rest and stop smoking – all of it easier said than done. To make matters worse, I had recently parted company with Diane and my self-confidence had taken a battering because another budding friendship had ended owing to irresolvable differences. I felt that I was destined never to enjoy a stable long-term relationship and, at almost 22 years of age, I feared that I was in danger of being 'left on the shelf'. Most of my cousins and many of my friends were 'going steady' and some were already married.

My self-esteem was restored by Caroline, an extremely good looking first year student of English, who was my close friend for the remainder of the summer term. My overriding desire for pretty girlfriends was undoubtedly a subconscious response to the observation that the most eligible of young men, both in my home village and at university, inevitably attracted the best-looking young women. Perhaps I considered the acquisition of such a girlfriend to be a measure of my own standing and a remedy for my lack of self-confidence. Unfortunately, the university contained many young men who were more likely to tempt an attractive young woman, although my involvement with the university's rock 'n' roll band gave me something of an added advantage.

Caroline was not confident about her own appearance because she was extremely conscious of a small scar on her face, the result of a childhood accident. Despite frequent reassurance that it was barely visible, she was always aware of its presence. In many ways I understood and sympathised because I too had a physical blemish that I feared might make me unattractive to the opposite sex. During my early childhood I had been laid low by a bad case of whooping cough, a fairly common illness during the 1940s and the 1950s, and the terrible cough that was a feature of the disease had distorted my rib cage because my bones were still undeveloped and pliable at the time. At grammar school, the shape of my rib cage had been the cause of some interest and much amusement among my fellow classmates, especially in the changing rooms for gym. To my intense embarrassment, when the school doctor made his yearly medical inspection, he usually commented, 'Ah, I can see that you have had whooping cough'. I needed no reminder of the fact so, wherever possible, I hid my deformity. In the summer, I always wore a shirt in public and sunbathed in private. I had yet to learn that my fears were irrational and that character and personality were more important than looks in any enduring relationship; good looks were a bonus and not a necessity. During my time with Caroline I learned one important and painful lesson. At the end of every evening we spent together at the university, one of her female flatmates would mysteriously arrive on the scene and relieve me of the task of escorting her back to their lodgings. When I commented on this, she laughed and explained that her friends disliked our association because they considered me to be irresponsible, reckless and untrustworthy, and were keeping a careful eye on the situation. It was a shock to discover that some fellow students thought of me in a way that was very different from the way I saw myself.

The start of the examination period finally arrived. The first Mathematics paper was a disaster. As I sat down in my designated place and spotted the paper on the desk, I was gripped with a feeling of total terror. I sat for a long time just staring at the paper with my stomach churning, my body trembling and sweat pouring down my face. My instinct was to run. It was well over a half an hour before I could control myself sufficiently to read the questions on the paper, but I was clearly in no state to perform at my best. The second examination in the afternoon was no better as I struggled to attempt some of the questions in between periods of intense and uncontrollable panic.

Luckily, there was a 10 day break before the History of Science examination papers and that enabled me to gain a measure of control over my emotions. When those papers were completed, I was confident that I had performed well, because my revision had focussed on the correct topics. Fearing the worst, I made an appointment with the tutor in charge of the course to discuss my problems regarding the mathematics papers. He told me that my distress during the mathematics examinations had been noticed and recorded but, in view of my limited responses to the questions, the Examination Board was likely to recommend that I should retake both papers again at a later date. Unfortunately, this was not possible until the May 1963 examinations, at the end of the next academic year. Meanwhile, in anticipation of this proposal he suggested that I should consider making arrangements for an enforced gap year. In due course, the results were declared and I was condemned to a one year wait before I could complete my degree and move on. Regrettably, a retake denied me the opportunity to begin studying for a Master's degree in History of Science in the coming September.

My failure to complete the course was a disaster and one that was hard to bear. I knew that my parents would be extremely disappointed, so I decided to stay in Leicester for the summer and negotiated with my landlord for an extension of the tenancy at Gopsall Street until the middle of August. Although I was officially no longer a student, my intention was to remain close by the university and to use its facilities for revision and entertainment. For the past three years, I had enjoyed living within the closed and privileged society of a university, and resolved to continue doing so until my degree was completed. I was well aware that eventually I would have to confront my parents and endure the inevitable inquest about my failure to finish the course. I knew that my mother would be tearful but supportive and that my father would be terse and berate me for wasting my time, his money and a golden opportunity for self-improvement that had been denied to his generation. Not surprisingly, I decided to delay this meeting for as long as I could. Meanwhile, I needed employment as my money had almost run out.

As a short term solution to my problem, I replied to an advertisement in the *Leicester Mercury* for weekend staff at the Old Horse Public House, situated opposite to the Victoria Park on London Road, close by the university and a popular drinking venue for students. During my interview with the manager it became obvious that he considered me to be totally unsuitable for the post that had been advertised, which involved serving behind the lounge bar and waiting on table in the adjoining restaurant. No doubt my long unwashed hair and stubbly beard did not convey the image that he

The Old Horse, London Road (circa 1960), a favourite haunt of students and the place where I was first introduced to 'Old Bill' and the joys of bar work. (K. Shepherdson)

was looking for. Nevertheless, almost as an afterthought, he asked if I would be willing to work at weekends in the public bar as an assistant to 'Old Bill', who had been seriously ill and needed help until he was fully recovered. As my financial position was critical, I had no alternative but to accept. And so, every Friday, Saturday and Sunday evenings for the following six or more weekends, I walked from Gopsall Street to the Old Horse to try my hand at being a barman.

Originally a 19th-century coaching inn, the Old Horse was a busy bay-fronted public house facing out onto Leicester's main London Road. Inside the main entrance there was a long through passage, from which a door immediately to the left led into a small public bar and another door to the right opened into a larger lounge/dining room with two bay windows looking out over Victoria Park. A door at the end of the passage led into the kitchen and storage areas. The public bar was simply furnished with five or six heavy circular iron tables, surrounded by numerous wooden chairs. The faded wooden floorboards showed clearly that they had been regularly scrubbed and the ceiling and cream coloured walls were dyed brown by years of exposure to tobacco smoke. At the far end of the room, opposite to its single bay window, was the bar where three hand pumps dispensed Everards ordinary, best and mild beers. Behind and below the bar, numerous shelves held bottles of pale and brown ale, stout, mixers and soft drinks. The fashion of the time was for draught and bottled beers, sometimes mixed together as a light or brown 'top'. Keg beer and lager were still as yet a novelty. Spirits were dispensed from optics suspended from the back wall. A central door to the rear of the bar led into a small storeroom which contained a large metal sink for washing glasses and ashtrays. From the side of the bar a small frosted glass window opened out onto the passage for off-licence sales.

Old Bill, a short, stocky, grey-haired and amiable man in his early 60s, was certainly in need of help. His illness had left him weak and short of breath, and it was hard for him to cope alone behind the bar, wheezing painfully as he shuffled from one customer to the next. Bill was a very experienced barman and in no time at all he taught me the fundamentals of bar-keeping, directing my activities while he sat on a stool. Most of the customers in the public bar were working-class men, mainly of Irish and Polish descent, who lived in the nearby rows of terraced houses on the outskirts of the suburb of Highfields. Arguments were common and some of them occasionally degenerated into fist fights, when Bill and I would tactfully withdraw into the backroom until differences were resolved and peace restored.

Most of the patrons at the Old Horse were exceedingly generous and frequently bought Bill and me drinks as part of their round. Unfortunately, we were never allowed to convert these treats into cash because most of the customers insisted that we should draw our beer immediately and begin drinking it in front of them. It was not unusual for both Bill and me to be pleasantly intoxicated by the end of an evening's service, when washing the glasses and cleaning the tables became an intolerable chore. On many occasions the used glasses were merely dunked into hot water in our haste to clear up and go home. Outside the bar, two long benches stood on either side of the passageway for customers to use while waiting for off-licence sales. These were regularly occupied by a group of elderly women who visited the public house in search of company and conversation over a bottle of stout or something stronger. They were mostly widows, dressed in fox fur stoles, flower-pot hats, long sombre dresses, granny boots and wrinkly thick stockings, and we served them through the side off-licence window. I became quite fond of our 'regular ladies' and I often joined them in the passage for a drink and a chat whenever I was not working.

However, my income from working at the Old Horse was not sufficient by itself to finance my everyday existence and so I still needed to find a regular weekday occupation. A few days after starting work at the Old Horse, I dialled the contact number I had been given by a friend for a local hospital that was in need of temporary domestic staff for the summer and was invited to attend for an interview with the hospital's Domestic Bursar the following afternoon. I arrived at the Leicester Royal Infirmary at the appointed time and presented myself at the reception desk. To my astonishment, as soon as the receptionist had contacted the Domestic Bursar to tell her that I had arrived, she informed me that the Bursar had no record of my telephone conversation and that my arrival was unexpected. As the Bursar was free and willing to see me, I was immediately directed along the corridor to her office and I was introduced to an apologetic Mrs Taylor-Brown.

Mrs Taylor-Brown, a neat well-manicured blonde lady in her early 40s, dressed impeccably in a white blouse, tweed suit and comfortable shoes, was clearly confused by my arrival. Her manner changed to laughter when I told her the reason why I was there and the telephone number that I had used. 'You are at the wrong hospital', she explained. The number that I had been given was for the Domestic Bursar at the Leicester General Hospital, not the Royal Infirmary. Up until that moment I did not know that Leicester had more than one large hospital. Luckily, Mrs Taylor-Brown was also in need of temporary staff to cover the summer holiday period and I was appointed to work from 7am until 4pm, Mondays to Fridays, for the duration of the summer as a general window-cleaner and to cover for absences among the teams of men

Leicester Royal Infirmary, Main Entrance circa 1960. Working at the hospital was a life changing experience for me. (University Hospitals of Leicester NHS Trust)

responsible for scrubbing the floors of the hospital's wards, corridors and offices, a lucky mistake that was to prove a life-changing event.

For most of that summer I cleaned windows at the hospital and occasionally I deputised on the scrubbing gangs. The task that I enjoyed the most was cleaning the windows in the Nurses' Home, not just because the sisters in charge regularly brought me tea and biscuits served on a silver tray, but also because there was always the chance that I might stumble across a nurse who was on the nightshift asleep in her bedroom. Among the other students working for the summer at the Leicester Royal Infirmary was Diane's friend, Liz. Liz hailed from South Africa and had been sent to England to study fashion at the Leicester Art and Tech by her father who owned a shirt making factory in Cape Town. One morning when I was cleaning the windows of the nurses' dining room, I spotted Liz approaching with a companion who she introduced to me as Celia. It transpired that Celia, a thin, pale-faced young Leicester woman with short dark hair dyed blonde at the front, was working at the hospital for the summer prior to joining a degree course in English at Trinity College, Dublin. I next met Celia when I was cleaning the windows of the Pathology Museum next to the Nurses' Home and she was cleaning and dusting inside. In this macabre location, surrounded by bottles and jars containing unrecognisable body parts suspended in formalin, we struck up a conversation and began what quickly became a close friendship. Within a few days, Liz announced that Celia was joining her in renting a flat in St James' Road for the summer. As this was just around the corner from the Old Horse public house and on my way home to Gopsall Street, it soon became a regular stopping-off place for a very necessary late-night sobering coffee and a brief rest after my hectic weekend shifts behind the bar.

Sunday 5 August 1962 was my 22nd birthday and, in desperate need of companionship, I invited Celia to join me at the nearby Taj-Mahal Indian restaurant for a late-night curry after my evening service at the Old Horse had ended, and to celebrate my birthday. At the restaurant I demonstrated my ignorance of Indian cuisine by ordering a chicken Madras for myself and a vegetable curry for Celia. The Taj-Mahal on Highfield Street was one of the first Indian restaurants to be established in Leicester and Asian cooking was a new experience for many students. My limited knowledge of Indian dishes was such that I believed simply that curry came in three different strengths: Korma, Madras and Vindaloo, the latter described as spicy hot, fiery and almost inedible. I have no doubt that the restaurateurs punished our ignorance by making most of these dishes far too hot for those English palates that were used mainly to relatively bland flavours. For Celia, who was a long-standing vegetarian, her first experience of Indian food was undoubtedly a disappointment, despite the consumption of several bottles of Indian beer.

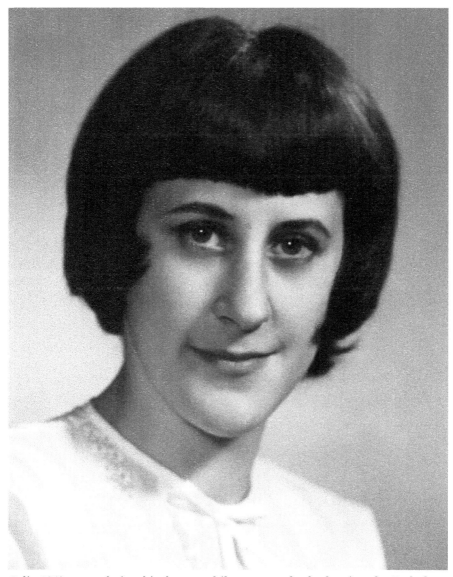

Celia 1963; our relationship began while we were both cleaning the Pathology Museum at Leicester Royal Infirmary.

My Madras was so heavily spiced that it burned my mouth and Celia's vegetable curry appeared to be an unappetising mixture of unrecognisable vegetables in a mild sandy-coloured sauce. Nevertheless, the evening was a great success and by the time it ended with coffee at St James' Road, what began as a friendship had turned into something much better. Thereafter, Celia willingly provided Old Bill and me with some very welcome assistance at clearing-up time in the Old Horse public bar.

The Evington Street/ Melbourne Road junction. Despite being regarded as an inner city slum, the area around Evington and Gopsall Streets was home to a vibrant multi-cultural community. (Source: Highfields Remembered, http://highfields.dmu.ac.uk.)

A few days after my birthday, Russ, my guitarist friend from the Incas, who was also spending the summer in Leicester, informed me that he had been given the option of hiring a house in Highfields which was large enough to provide accommodation for up to five students for the next academic year. Consequently, he was looking for four more students to rent the house with him. As independent student accommodation was becoming extremely difficult to find and my Gopsall Street tenancy was about to end, I quickly volunteered to join him. Liz and Celia were also keen to move having found their St James' Road flat to be neither as convenient nor as comfortable as they had originally thought. So, from 11 August, the four of us took up residence in a house at 40 Evington Street in Highfields. An artist acquaintance from the Art and Tech became the fifth member of the household and Russ' friend Roy, a third year geologist, volunteered to take Celia's place when she eventually began her course in Dublin.

40 Evington Street was a once impressive bay-fronted Victorian terraced house that had seen better days and was now in dire need of renovation. Owned by a middle-aged Polish couple, the property not only provided them with a generous income from its student tenants but also with accommodation for their elderly father, who used the large downstairs front lounge as a bed-sitting room. Mr Mikulski, a tall and once handsome elderly gentleman, spoke very little English and spent most of his time out of the house visiting his relatives or meeting friends at a nearby Polish club. When he was at home, he made very little use of the facilities in the house and spent most of his time locked inside his front room accommodation. Living in a shared residence with five noisy students was most probably not the most pleasurable experience but, nevertheless, it was an experience that he endured with good grace. On the few occasions that we met, he smiled and attempted to make friendly conversation in a mixture of Polish and broken English, embellished by many hand-signals, grunts and facial contortions.

The accommodation at 40 Evington Street was quite spacious. A path led from the main street through a small garden to the front door which opened in onto a long passageway. Immediately to the left was the front room used by Mr Mikulski and next to this was a small communal lounge furnished with a dusty three piece suite, a sideboard, numerous stick-back chairs and a coffee table. At the end of the corridor there was a small dining room with a table and chairs and, beyond this, a communal kitchen equipped simply with a gas cooker, Belfast sink and two larder cupboard units. From the kitchen a back door opened out into a large walled and paved backyard in which stood an outbuilding consisting of an outside flush lavatory, a shed and a redundant coal store. At the end of the yard was a disused two-storey workshop with wooden steps on the outside leading up from the yard to the first floor offices.

From the ground floor corridor, stairs led up to a first floor landing, off which doors opened into three bedrooms that were furnished to be used as one double and two single bed-sitting rooms. There was also a communal bathroom furnished with a chipped enamelled metal bath, a sink and a flush toilet, with hot water supplied by a large, noisy and extremely temperamental gas water-heater. A further staircase led up to a single attic room. Although every room had a fireplace, all the flues were filled with old newspapers and sacking, indicating clearly that they had not been used for some time. The only heating throughout the whole of the house was provided by two small portable electric fires. As soon as we had moved in, the four of us established ourselves as residents in the rooms on the first floor, while our artist friend converted the attic into a temporary studio.

For most of the remaining summer, Liz, Celia and I worked at the hospital during the day, while I also continued serving behind the bar of the Old Horse at weekends. Russ was less fortunate, because the only weekly employment he could find was on the late-night shift at a bakery in Uppingham. After work we played cards, read books or strummed our guitars and sang in the evening sun before Russ left for the bakery on his Vespa scooter and we made our way to bed. Our artist friend rarely joined us in these revels, preferring to spend most of his time alone painting and sculpting in his studio, while his presence was indicated solely by the frequent paint and plaster-of-Paris trails from the back yard, where he mixed his materials, to his attic accommodation. Occasionally he was joined in the attic by his girlfriend, who allegedly posed in the nude for his life drawings. It was a time for relaxing and recharging our batteries after the many traumas of the previous few months. During that time, my relationship with Celia grew stronger and, in true romantic fashion, we even adopted a popular recording that we called our song, a summertime favourite of 1962, *Sealed with a Kiss*, by Brian Hyland.

CHAPTER 13

TWO GUITARS IN DENMARK

Towards the end of August, Rod arrived to spend a few days with us at Evington Street, as he and I were soon to leave on a hiking trip to Denmark that we had planned many months before. Not that I was as keen to go now since my circumstances had changed. Celia was due to leave for Dublin at the end of September and two weeks or more travelling on the Continent were precious weeks lost from our remaining time together. On Monday 20 August, after leaving my summer jobs at the Old Horse and the Royal Infirmary, Rod and I set out to hitchhike along the A47 to Norfolk so that I could collect my passport from my home in Rollesby and meet once again with my parents. Rod's company meant that I was less apprehensive about that meeting than if I had been alone.

The journey began badly and we waited for almost two hours before we were given our first lift. No doubt the sight of two rather dishevelled young men, heavily laden with kitbag, haversack and two guitars, was sufficient to deter most motorists from stopping to give us a ride. Our first lift was provided by a young commercial traveller who was travelling to a lunch appointment at a public house in Rutland. As a result, we found ourselves at a small roadside inn on the A47 close to Uppingham that advertised itself as 'The first inn in Rutland', where Rod and I spent a happy hour talking while drinking a lunchtime pint or two of beer. Our fortunes suddenly changed after we left the inn when we were offered a lift in a lorry owned by Lanham and Sons, hauliers from Little Ormesby, a Norfolk village a mere mile away from my Rollesby home. Three hours later, we arrived at my family home on the Martham Road in time for tea and the long-delayed meeting with my parents. Luckily, I had no need to worry on that score as they were happy in the knowledge that I was now clear about my future intentions. They also believed strongly that having to undertake menial work for a year might prove to be a salutary experience for me. I had taken too many things for granted and failed to make the best of the opportunities that a university education had offered. They wisely suggested that a year at work might focus my mind on the future, rather than the past. After a good meal, Rod and I practiced on our guitars while my mother and father listened approvingly.

The next day, we bade a sad farewell to my parents and began thumbing for a lift to London. In no time at all we had been picked up by a passing lorry and arrived in

London three hours later. After Rod had collected clean clothes from his London home, we travelled by train to Dover, where we boarded the late night ferry to Ostend in Belgium. Our preparations had been more meticulous than those I had made for my previous year's trip to Austria. We had both joined the Youth Hostel Association, packed a blanket and sheet for emergency bedding and had checked that our arrival on the Continent did not coincide with any national public holidays. But, as both of us were wearing jeans, a sweater, heavy jacket and suede shoes, we were still inappropriately dressed for hiking.

Our intention was to travel through Belgium and Germany to Copenhagen in Denmark, where we had been invited to stay at the family home of Rod's Danish girlfriend, Ulla. On our journey, we were picked up outside of Antwerp by a Dutch businessman on his way to Eindhoven, who chatted to us in perfect English. Having commented on his excellent command of the English language, he told us that he owed this to the fact that he had an English wife. It further transpired that his wife was born in Great Yarmouth and, on discovering that I came from a village near to Great Yarmouth, he excitedly decided that we should return home with him to meet his wife and reminisce with her about her old home town. Unfortunately, his home was in Amsterdam and not on our proposed route to Denmark, yet with little hesitation we both accepted his kind invitation. And so, after a brief business stop in Eindhoven, we spent our first night on the Continent not in Germany as expected but on a diversion through Holland.

In Amsterdam, we were taken to our Dutch host's home where we were introduced to his wife and teenage daughter, who were most surprised to meet two unexpected guests. Despite our unexpected arrival, we were made very welcome and provided with a room in which to spread out our bedding. Having spent the previous night awake busking on the deck of the overnight ferry, Rod and I were exhausted. So, after a pleasant meal washed down by numerous glasses of lager, we entertained our hosts with a folk song or two before rudely falling fast asleep on their sofa. During the meal, we discovered that our host's daughter was an ardent fan of Cliff Richard and, as a gesture of thanks for their hospitality and to apologise for our tiredness, when we eventually returned home to England I sent her the autographed photograph that Cliff Richard had given me during the previous RAG week.

On leaving Amsterdam, we continued travelling northwards, and eventually on to Denmark, with overnight stops at youth hostels in Emden, Hamburg and Aabenraa, the latter just inside Denmark. We were regularly picked up by private individuals and businessmen in large cars who were keen to advertise the achievements of their region

Rod and me on our way to Denmark, August 1962.

and country, more often than not in perfect English. On the approach to Bremen, one such businessman was so preoccupied with showing Rod and me the evidence of German economic recovery in the surrounding countryside that he lost concentration and drove into the rear of the car in front. Fortunately nobody was seriously hurt. The only casualty was my front tooth, which was chipped when my head hit the dashboard. But his vehicle was so badly dented that it was temporarily immobilised, so we thanked him for his generosity and tactfully left him on the roadside, engaged in an earnest conversation with a traffic policeman.

In Hamburg, we spent the night at the main youth hostel, which was located in the centre of the city close to the infamous red-light district of the Reeperbahn. The temptation to explore the Reeperbahn was far too great for us to resist and so we decided to spend an hour or more walking around the area in order to assess whether its reputation was well deserved. We saw numerous seedy club entrances, a great deal

On the approach to Bremen, this kind German businessman was so preoccupied with showing Rod and me the evidence of German economic recovery in the surrounding countryside that he lost concentration and drove into the rear of the car in front. (R. Davies)

Two guitars and one hiker arrive in Copenhagen, August 1962.

of gaudy advertising and numerous photographs of scantily clad young women, and ran the gauntlet of females touting for customers. But the sex industry was not the only entertainment on show. We were surprised to see that many of the regular performers at the Top Ten Club and similar venues in Hamburg were rock 'n' roll bands from England. At the time, the Beatles had not yet become established in Britain and their German exploits were not well known outside of Liverpool.

After three days on the road we finally arrived in Copenhagen late in the afternoon of Sunday 26 August and we spent the night at a youth hostel so that we could refresh ourselves before meeting Ulla and her family on the Monday. Ulla, Rod's Danish girlfriend, a strikingly good-looking Scandinavian blonde, was the daughter of a Danish government minister and so for the next six days we were entertained royally at their impressive residence in the Bagsværd suburb of Copenhagen. On those occasions when Ulla was at work or otherwise engaged, Rod and I were left to explore Copenhagen on our own, but in the evenings, while Ulla and Rod spent time alone together, I usually stayed behind to watch television with her family. Not that this posed any great difficulty for me as Danish television was then comprised mainly of British and American programmes with Danish subtitles.

During the following week Rod and I sampled most of Copenhagen's tourist attractions, including the famous Tivoli Gardens where, for the Danish equivalent of just two shillings, we attended a smouldering matinee performance given by my mother's favourite singer, Eartha Kitt, the aptly named 'sex kitten'. We were also keen to discover whether the Scandinavian reputation for sexual openness was true so, in a fit of daring, we paid the admission fee to a seedy looking cinema which had posters at its entrance showing photographs and drawings of naked men and women. Unfortunately, the feature film was not an example of rampant Scandinavian pornography, as we had hoped, but a British Health and Efficiency documentary with

Rod, me, Ulla and a friend enjoy a Danish beer or two.

Danish subtitles depicting daily life in a British nudist colony. To make matters worse, I had already seen the film at the Cameo cinema in Leicester.

At the weekend, after a dinner given in our honour by Ulla's parents and during which we gorged ourselves on smorgasbord and stew served with redcurrant jam, we played folk music on our guitars to entertain our new friends and they recorded our performance on a recently acquired tape-recorder. We said goodbye to Ulla and her family the next day and made our way to the docks, where we caught the ferry to Malmö in Sweden. Our intention was to hike around the Swedish countryside for a few days before making our way back home to England. Unfortunately, once we had arrived in Sweden, our fortunes took a turn for the worse. Everything seemed to be progressing very well when we were given a lift by two attractive young women who spoke reasonably good English. They gave us a brief motor tour around the city of Malmö while we serenaded them with guitar music from the back seats of their car. They then agreed to take us to the nearest local youth hostel, but when we arrived there we discovered a large notice pinned to the main door announcing that the building was closed for renovation and that the nearest alternative hostel accommodation was at Helsinborg, 40 kilometres further along the coast road. Our two new friends were kind enough to take us some 10 or more kilometres in the direction of Helsinborg, where we said goodbye and set off walking towards our destination.

The coast road between Malmö and Helsinborg was extremely picturesque in the evening sun, with views across the sea towards Denmark on one side and rolling hills covered in a dense forest on the other. Not that we were inclined to appreciate the scenery. Late evening was not the most ideal time to hitchhike because the road was virtually deserted and the cars that did pass by totally ignored our increasingly frantic attempts to obtain a lift. We discovered later that, in Sweden, hitchhikers were considered to be undesirable beggars and rarely offered lifts. As dusk descended, we had no option but to walk some way into the rapidly darkening forest, unroll our sheets and blankets to spend a very uncomfortable and cold night dozing fitfully on the hard ground. Early the next morning, we managed to obtain a lift from a passing van and arrived cold, tired and very irritable at Helsinborg where, totally disenchanted with Sweden, we caught the next available ferry back to Helsingor and hitchhiker-friendly Denmark.

For the next three days we slowly hiked our way back homewards through Demark, Germany, Holland and Belgium, arriving at Ostend late in the afternoon of Wednesday 5 September. Most of our overnight stays were spent at various youth hostels that provided us with cheap and clean bed and breakfast accommodation, although the sleeping quarters were usually communal dormitories furnished with numerous bunk beds. Residents were also expected to perform various cleaning duties before leaving in the morning. While most were small and friendly establishments, many German Jugendherberge were very large and frequently overcrowded. Youth hostelling was a national pastime for many young people in Germany during their summer break.

On our journey homewards, we arrived once more in Hamburg too late to find lodgings at the main youth hostel as it was already full, so we were directed to an overflow establishment, which turned out to be a large converted warehouse filled with row upon row of bunk beds. As we were still tired from our night in the forest, we quickly fell asleep, only to be woken shortly afterwards by the arrival of a large German youth group who proceeded to sing rousing songs well into the night, conducted by an overweight group leader dressed in lederhosen. Our frequent and often impolite shouts of disapproval were drowned out by the noise of their singing.

After an overnight stop at a Dutch family run youth hostel in Delden we arrived back at Ostend, both of us suffering from feverish colds (undoubtedly the legacy of our night in the forest) and there we bought tickets for the next night ferry to Dover. During the crossing we spent most of the night on deck, coughing, snuffling, playing our guitars and providing free entertainment for anyone who was inclined to listen. Back in England and tired of hiking, we travelled by train to London and then on again to Leicester, arriving at 40 Evington Street late that Thursday evening to an enthusiastic and extremely warm welcome.

CHAPTER 14

JOHNNY ANGEL AND THE MYSTICS

In many ways, the disbanding of Aztec and the Incas was a great disappointment to Russ and me. While we enjoyed playing acoustic guitar accompaniments and harmonising to Everly Brothers songs in our Evington Street back yard, our electric guitars and amplifiers were laying redundant in our bedrooms. So it was no surprise to the rest of the household when, in early September, we replied to an advertisement in the *Leicester Mercury* for rhythm and bass guitarists to join a local Leicester band. A few days later we arrived at 17 Crown Hills Rise, a small terraced house in the east of the city, which was the home of Alan Makin and his widowed mother. After a brief interview with three young rock musicians, Dougie, Alan and Bazzie, we agreed to join their recently formed rock 'n' roll band that performed under the name of 'Johnny Angel and the Mystics'. Dougie, a street-wise ex-Teddy Boy and market trader in his mid-20s, was a natural showman and an excellent singer in the style of Elvis Presley. Alan, a youthful 17-year-old office clerk, was the talented musician of the group and was proficient with both the piano and the guitar, while Bazzie, Alan's boyhood friend and neighbour, could competently bash out the rhythm for most rock 'n' roll numbers on his basic drum kit.

Their existing equipment was variable. Dougie's microphone was relayed through a home-made amplifier that appeared to be comprised mainly of parts salvaged from an old radio. Alan, on the other hand, played an expensive bright red Fender Stratocaster linked to a 30 watt Vox AC30 amplifier, while Bazzie's drum kit consisted solely of a bass drum, snare and cymbal. However, once supplemented by the equipment owned by Russ and me, the group made a considerable noise especially when practicing in Alan's small front room. Because the groups repertoire was almost identical to that of the Incas (mainly Cliff Richard numbers, Shadows instrumentals and covers of hit recordings from the current popular music charts) we quickly managed to put together a competent musical programme. Our first public performance was at the end of September at a sparsely attended dance for the South East Leicester Youth Club in the Assembly Rooms on Uppingham Road, followed immediately by a Saturday dance at the Leicester Art and Tech. The instrumentalists in the group adopted a uniform of black trousers, white shirts and blue ties for performances; but Dougie, in the persona of Johnny Angel, strutted his stuff in a gold lamé suit, red frilly shirt and white winkle-picker shoes, his elaborate Tony Curtis hairstyle held in place with Brylcreem and his face plastered thick with stage make-up.

An unforeseen problem arose when Aztec and the Incas were persuaded to perform for one last time at the university's 1962 Integration Hop, because all the members of the group were still resident in Leicester and linked in some way to the university: Rod on a Post-Graduate teacher training course; Trevor, Russ and Eric in the third year of their degree studies; and myself undergoing a gap year between examinations. With the minimum of preparation we played an hour long spot to a sea of new faces and old friends rocking and rolling on the Queen's Hall dance floor. For Rod, Trevor and Eric, this was their last performance with the group before settling down to serious studies. After leaving the Incas Rod continued his musical interests by performing at the university and various venues in town as a bluesy folk singer, while Eric returned to his first love, jazz, as the drummer in the university's jazz band.

But for Russ and me, the Inca story had not yet finished. Immediately following the Integration Hop, Russ was approached by Dave Jacobs, a newly arrived post-graduate student and a skilful pianist and guitarist, who was interested in joining a rock 'n' roll band. After some discussion, we re-launched the university's rock 'n' roll band for the 1962–63 academic year under the shortened title of the Incas, with Dave as lead guitarist, Russ on rhythm, a drummer called Charlie and myself on bass. As Rod was unavailable, Russ took over the role of singer as well as rhythm guitarist. For the duration of the university year, we performed in the intervals at many Saturday dances as well as at venues throughout the city, dressed entirely in black with our trousers held up by bright yellow braces.

With the Incas reformed Russ resigned immediately from the Mystics, putting that group's development on hold until a new rhythm guitarist could be found. I persisted with both bands, because together they provided me with a very welcome and much needed additional income. For a few months I was able to play for both groups without any conflict of interest. Eventually, a young 17-year-old rhythm guitarist, yet another guitar-playing Dave, joined the Mystics and rehearsals began again in earnest. Ron, Alan's older cousin, assumed the role of manager and booking agent, and began to seek engagements for the band. In style, Johnny Angel and the Mystics became clones of Cliff Richard and the Shadows, covering most of their current and past recordings and performing similarly intricate dance movements while we played our guitars. By Christmas we had put together an extremely competent programme of music that Ron was able to sell to potential venues. Alan was a very good guitar player in the style of Hank Marvin and so our gigs usually began with Shadows' instrumentals including

Apache, *FBI* and *Wonderful Land*, followed by various Cliff Richard numbers sung by Dougie – *Move it*, *Do You Wanna Dance*, *Theme for a Dream* and Cliff's current 1962 hit recording *It'll Be Me*, interspersed with hit songs by other artists including Johnny Kidd's *Shakin' All Over* and Chubby Checker's *Lets Twist Again*. The finale of the show was always a brief but exhausting instrumental adaptation of the *William Tell Overture*, played while performing high-kicks can-can style.

On my return from Denmark, I had resumed working at the hospital and, as I needed long-term employment for my gap year, I approached Mrs Taylor-Brown to see if a vacancy was available in her department until the following Easter, when I hoped to be able to stop work and revise for my outstanding degree examinations. Luckily she was pleased with my efforts during the summer and was happy to offer me a place on one of the hospital's floor-scrubbing teams. The pay was not good, just £10 a week, but employment from 7am until 4pm gave me sufficient time to play in the evenings with the bands. Once Celia had left Leicester for her degree course in Dublin, my time was filled almost entirely by work, playing and rehearsing with both the Incas and the Mystics, and, of course, revision.

My time at the hospital was everything that my parents hoped it would be. I had spent three years in the isolated community of a university and only now, thanks to my time at the Old Horse, my meeting with Celia and her family, playing with the Mystics and working at the hospital, was I at last coming in contact with the working people of Leicester and appreciating their problems, difficulties, thoughts and aspirations. I was surprised to discover that most of them held a very low opinion of the university, its staff and its students. My companions on the scrubbing team were Albert and Derek. Albert, a short stocky moustachioed man in his early 50s and the leader of our team, was a working-class intellectual. His knowledge of politics, world affairs and current social issues, gleaned through reading newspapers and listening intently to the radio, was embarrassingly better than my own. Had he received the advantage of a good education, then he would certainly not have been employed as a poorly paid domestic servant in a hospital. Derek, despite his youthful looks, was in his early 40s. A casualty of the war, Derek was clearly brain-

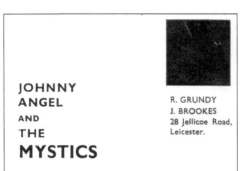

Advertising Johnny Angel and the Mystics.

damaged and had a steel plate covering a large hole in his skull, the consequence of being blown up by a bomb. For most of the time, Derek was a quiet and amiable companion who worked hard without complaint, but at times he was troubled and agitated by severe headaches which he attributed to wireless signals sent by the Prime Minister from Downing Street as punishment for things that he had done wrong. No kind words could convince him otherwise.

As one of four or more scrubbing teams, we were responsible for cleaning the floors of all the corridors, wards and consulting rooms in the hospital. From 7.00 until 9.00 in the morning we cleaned corridors, offices and, once a week, the outpatients department, before most of the medical and office staff arrived. After a short tea-break, the remainder of the working day was spent cleaning one of the six major wards in the hospital, together with various consulting rooms and treatment theatres. Albert was in charge of the scrubbing machine, while Derek and I followed behind with two large mops to dry the scrubbed floor. When dirty, the mops were rinsed clean in a mobile tank of hot water and wrung out through a mangle attached to one of its ends. Working on the wards was an emotional experience. It was necessary to move all the beds so that we could scrub the floors underneath them and, while doing so, it was possible to converse and joke with the recovering patients, but it was difficult to know how to address the seriously ill and dying. It was the first time in my short life that I had come face to face with illness and death, and encountered people with difficulties and challenges far more serious than anything I had ever experienced.

Death was a taboo subject for my parents and was considered an inappropriate topic for discussion. Despite my Grandfather Miller's total commitment to the Church of England, neither of my parents professed strong religious views. In her youth my mother was a Sunday school teacher, but it seems that the horror of wartime had dented her faith, as it had for many of her generation. On one memorable occasion, she informed me that she could not believe in a God, or a heaven and a hell. She considered that paradise existed here on Earth if we would only take the time to stop fighting and look for it. Death was a final end to life rather than a portal to a new existence in her opinion and an event not to be contemplated in advance. Yet, as a child, I was encouraged to attend Sunday school and I was a regular member of the Rollesby Church choir until my teens. Few of my university friends displayed any religious commitment; although most of them were agnostics and only a few were atheists. Inevitably, in an environment where we were encouraged to question all things, it became clear to many of us that knowledge was mainly a set of possibilities and probabilities, while certainty was a matter of faith.

Until 1957 my only experience of death was the passing of a much loved family pet. My first experience of the death of a close family relative was when my Grandmother Miller died suddenly in May 1957 on my mother's birthday. In the early hours of the morning, she suffered a massive stroke, the consequence of an aneurysm, and, as she lay dying, grandfather summoned the family. Despite the fact that I was 16 years of age, neither of my parents would tell me what was happening until after she had died. I was left sleeping in my bed while they attended her bedside. They also insisted that I went to school on the day of her funeral. Like most of my peers, I was protected by my parents from the trauma of death, so much so that we grew up with the notion that death was a problem only for the old and not for the young, an attitude that has persisted to this day. My work at the hospital rapidly dispelled this myth and demonstrated all too clearly the fragility of life. Soon after I began working at the Infirmary, I was informed that a friend from the university, a young woman with a liking for motorcycles, had been admitted following an accident on her motorbike. When I asked if I could visit her, the Sister in charge of the accident ward gently informed me that my friend had just died from her injuries.

Living at Evington Street during the infamous winter of 1962–63 was no pleasure at all. The two electric fires were of little use in warming the house so, when we were at home, we all spent most of the time in bed. It was not unusual to find six or more people top to toe in one bed, fully dressed, three in the top and three along the bottom, talking, playing cards or drinking coffee to keep warm. At night, everyone slept under a pile of blankets, often supplemented by overcoats and odd articles of clothing. The insides of the window panes were regularly frosted over by ice. Mostly, we ate our food in the kitchen huddled around a lit burner on the gas stove, the walls running wet with condensation. One evening we discovered that the pipes had burst in the outside lavatory and that the water overflowing onto the toilet floor had frozen, making it impossible to open the door. Fortunately we were able to turn off the lavatory's water supply because there was a stopcock in the kitchen and the toilet in the bathroom meant that the occupants of the house had alternative facilities. Only once did we try to light a fire in one of the grates. While I was ill in bed with a flu-like cold, Russ and Roy bought some coal and lit a fire in my room to keep me warm. They had removed all the paper and debris that they could see, but the flue was still blocked and my room was filled with smoke.

If the summer of 1962 was a low point in my life then the summer of 1963 was a vast improvement. My examination retakes at the end of May went smoothly, although my expectations of success were low. On the day that the results were declared I did not hurry to the university to find out if I had successfully obtained a degree. It was Roy who brought

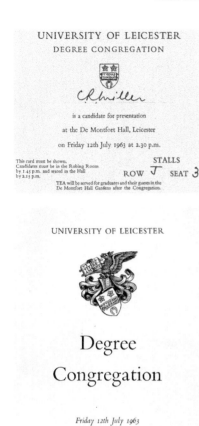

UNIVERSITY OF LEICESTER
DEGREE CONGREGATION

C.R.Miller

is a candidate for presentation

at the De Montfort Hall, Leicester

on Friday 12th July 1963 at 2.30 p.m.

This card must be shown.
Candidates must be in the Robing Room
by 1.45 p.m. and seated in the Hall
by 2.15 p.m.

STALLS

ROW *J*   SEAT *3*

TEA will be served for graduates and their guests in the
De Montfort Hall Gardens after the Congregation.

UNIVERSITY OF LEICESTER

Degree
Congregation

Friday 12th July 1963

Graduation, July 1963.

me the unexpected news that I had obtained a lower second-class honours degree. Because I had retaken two of my final papers, I had expected just a pass or a third-class degree at best. My parents were elated by the news and, two weeks later, drove in my father's ancient car all the way from Norfolk to Leicester for the awards ceremony, the furthest that my father had driven since the end of World War Two. With my degree completed, I successfully applied to the Faculty of Education to join September's post-graduate teacher training course and began what eventually resulted in a long and happy career teaching mathematics in various further and higher education establishments. Most of my training took place in a Leicestershire comprehensive middle-school managed according to the county's Mason Plan, a comprehensive system developed by the county's Chief Education Officer. I applauded the underlying idealism and socialist principles of the comprehensive system in theory, but I quickly realised that I had been lucky to receive a grammar school education, despite its apparent middle-class bias. It seemed to me at the time that, no matter what their background, under the comprehensive scheme the more able children were often unchallenged and bored, while the presence of teenage girls was a serious distraction for the boys, one that I would have found extremely difficult to cope with.

My love life had also taken a turn for the better. Thanks to a generous contribution from the Mystics' swear box, a well-used feature of band rehearsals, I was able to afford a weekend visit in February to see Celia at Trinity College in Dublin. The visit opened my eyes to a very different style of university, one definitely based on the Oxbridge model, an environment in which I was truly uncomfortable. Even the music was different. At a Saturday dance, we were entertained by an excellent Irish show-band that provided a welcome change from the rock 'n' roll groups that were beginning to dominate Saturday dances in Leicester. My visit was a great success because it cemented my relationship with

Sir Bazil Spence addresses students at my 1963 graduation ceremony in the De Montfort Hall, Leicester. (Leicester Mercury Media Group).

Celia and, when she returned to Leicester for the Easter vacation, we decided to get married at some point in the future. Obstacles that had ended other relationships almost before they had begun – those irresolvable differences based on circumstances, prejudice and indecision – had failed to separate us and those difficulties that did occur were proved to be solvable with a little perseverance. Because Celia was only just 19 years old, she was considered legally underage and it was imperative that I gained her parents' consent before we were able to marry. Once this was obtained, we were married on Saturday 17 August 1963 at the Registry Office in Leicester.

A few days before the wedding, I moved into the single room that Russ had occupied at Evington Street, because he had left Leicester after graduating in June. The accommodation was very basic and both sets of parents were horrified that we were starting married life in such cramped conditions. The room that we shared with a family of mice was furnished simply with a double bed, a large wardrobe and a chest of drawers. Celia's father provided two additional armchairs that he had bought second-hand in a sale and Celia's mother attempted to improve the look of the room by arriving one evening with wallpaper and paint, intent on decorating our small accommodation. My parents first visited Evington Street when they arrived in Leicester on the day before our wedding, their second trip to Leicester in just over a month. As ill-luck would have it, they arrived during a rain storm and because the guttering above the front door was broken, they were drenched as they rang the doorbell. To make matters worse, the door was opened by Mr Mikulski, who did not know who they were and told them to go away in a mixture of broken English and Polish. Luckily, I managed to rescue them and welcomed them in, dripping wet and thoroughly confused.

Saturday 17 August was a fine summer day. Before changing for the 11.15am ceremony at the Registry Office on Pocklington's Walk, I made a brief trip into the city centre and used some of the £20 that my parents had given me as a wedding present to purchase a small coffee table and the must-have of the moment, a small silver and blue portable battery-powered transistor radio with an extendable aerial, a surprise gift for Celia. At 10am, dressed formally in my charcoal grey suit, I was collected by Celia's father and we spent so much time gathering courage at the White Swan public house in the Market Place, that we were nearly late for the ceremony. Afterwards Celia and I dined with both sets of parents at the Belmont Hotel in Leicester and ended the day at my new in-laws' house in Braunstone for cake and champagne. In the early evening we bade them all goodbye and went to the Old Horse for a private celebratory drink. Because I had purchased the radio, I had taken the unusual precaution of locking the door to the room. During the excitement of the day I had lost the key and we had to break the lock on the door to get inside, much to the amusement of the other residents in the house. Our wedding presents

Saturday 17 August 1963. Our limited finances ensured a small Registry Office wedding and a return to work on the Monday.

Humberstone Gate, Leicester. For a while, Celia worked in Lewis' cash office high up in the iconic tower of their Leicester department store.

consisted of two linen bed-sheets, a Pyrex dinner service, a tea set and five casserole dishes. We had no money to spend on a honeymoon so we both returned to our holiday jobs at the Royal Infirmary on the following Monday.

Soon after we were married, Celia became seriously ill and spent some time in hospital. Regrettably, she was not sufficiently recovered in time to start her second year of study at Trinity and was obliged to withdraw from the course. In many ways her disappointment was a mixed blessing because, as a result, we were not forced to endure the regular separations that we had anticipated while she completed her studies in Dublin. Because of illness and the need to earn a living, it was another 10 years before she was able to restart her studies at university. Once she had recovered sufficiently, she took a temporary job in the finance department at Lewis' department store on Humberstone Gate. Together with the grant that I received as a teacher in training plus the money I earned from part-time employment and playing with the Mystics, Celia's small income was sufficient to enable us to leave Evington Street in the spring of 1964 and move to a more salubrious ground floor flat on Brazil Street, close to the Leicester City Football Club's Filbert Street ground. Our well-furnished new flat consisted of a lounge, double bedroom, dining room, kitchen and lean-to toilet. Outside there was a small back yard with a clothes line. Although this was a great improvement on 40 Evington Street, our use of the upstairs bathroom that we shared with the occupants of the first floor flat was restricted to one bath each per week.

Chapter 15

Out on the Town

Despite the many setbacks that occurred during my studies at university, the late 1950s and early 1960s were exciting times for me, just as they were for most of my contemporaries. Many people in my parents' and grandparents' generations had become addicted to television and now preferred to stay at home rather than go out to the dance hall and the cinema, a situation that opened the way for the development of leisure-time activities aimed specifically for the young. By the mid to late 1950s Britain was gradually emerging from a period of dull, restrictive post-war austerity and was slowly entering a phase of almost full employment. More teenagers were entering the world of work at the age of 16 than were electing to stay in further education. As a result, most ordinary young men and women had more money in their pockets than ever before to spend on entertainment and fashions. The advent of rock 'n' roll, the adverse reaction by many older people to its primitive beat and the rebellious attitudes portrayed in the cinema by the likes of James Dean and Marlon Brando, fuelled the natural desire of most young people to be different from and more exciting than their parents.

It was inevitable that astute businessmen and women would provide many opportunities in the fields of commerce and leisure for young people to spend this new found wealth and to express their need to be different in fashionable clothes, new technology, loud music and entertainments aimed specifically at the young. Those of us who remained in higher education were certainly disadvantaged by the absence of a regular weekly wage. For some students maintenance grants were generous, but they still failed to match the incomes of those at work, although holiday employment did much to help close that gap. Fortunately, the subsidised activities at the Students' Union, together with a general tendency among most students to spend the money in their pockets on entertainment rather than subsistence, ensured that we made full use of the locally available leisure facilities although, for most, fashionable and expensive clothes were unaffordable.

Before university, I had little understanding of fashion. At home, I was dressed by my mother at her expense and my clothes were similar in style to those of my father. School uniforms were quite expensive and they needed to be regularly replaced. Consequently, there was little money left for other clothes and my casual wear was often made up from redundant items of my school uniform (grey trousers, grey shirt, red and black striped tie, sleeveless grey pullover, black blazer with the Great Yarmouth coat of arms on the breast pocket, black mackintosh, grey socks and black lace-up shoes) with a sports jacket as an alternative to the blazer. A smart suit was an essential acquisition once I began to attend dances. My first suit was bought for me by my Grandmother Miller as a 15th birthday present, a personally designed two-piece suit in a powder blue cloth with a red check, tailor-made by Burton's of Great Yarmouth. The jacket was double breasted with two vents at the back and large pointed revers. The trousers, held up by a pair of my father's braces, had 24-inch bottoms, turn-ups and a buttoned fly. A white shirt with a blue woollen tie completed the ensemble although, in cold weather, I also wore a grey pullover under the jacket, normally a sleeveless pullover with a cable stitch pattern that had been knitted at home by my mother. I was proud of my suit despite the fact that when I wore it I looked more like a colourful gangster from the 1930s than a fashionable teenager of the 1950s.

By the late-1950s, I had become more fashion conscious and was able to follow the current trends because my casual earnings during school holidays increased, providing me with a modest surplus of cash with which to indulge my whims. I was definitely tired of grey and greatly admired the colourful clothing of the Teddy Boys, although I persuaded my parents that I deplored their behaviour. Narrow trousers with 14-inch bottoms were the height of fashion, but I could never convince my mother to take in my 24-inch bottomed school trousers. I was also very much attracted by the off-duty wear worn by the many American servicemen who visited Great Yarmouth to drink and relax in the seafront bars. So I imitated them and adopted colourful jumpers and canvas baseball boots as my casual wear, not always to my mother's liking. Many of my more garishly patterned Saturday purchases were taken back to the shop by my mother and exchanged for a more subdued selection. I adored slip-on shoes and was amazed when members of the sixth form were given permission to wear them for school. Unfortunately, I preferred wearing slip-on shoes with colourful socks, not the normal sombre grey. For a while white socks were ignored but once the fashionable trend was for luminous lime green and shocking pink socks, the headmaster called a halt and introduced a ban on all colourful socks. Influenced by the fashions of the traditional jazz fans, at university I started wearing corduroy and cavalry twill trousers, suede shoes and long jumpers; a fashion that had my mother's full approval. In the winter I wore a duffle coat. I also wore striped collarless shirts that I cadged from my Grandfather, sometimes adding a stiff white collar attached to the shirt by studs, but more often than not with no collar at all, and never with a tie.

After I had seen the film *Rock around the Clock* I became more conscious of my hairstyle. Bill Haley wore his hair long and swept back, with the front combed to form a curl over his forehead, appropriately known as his kiss-curl. Like many other teenage boys, I grew my hair longer and spent many hours in front of a mirror trying to train my hair to look like Bill Haley's. Up until then, my hair was cut in the same way as my father's, a short back and sides. Every two weeks, my father and I visited the village barber's shop where my hair was clipped short, almost to the skin, up to an inch above the ears, the top thinned with scissors and comb, then plastered with a handful of Brylcreem and combed to each side with a perfectly straight off-centre parting. When Elvis Presley became popular, my Bill Haley hairstyle was modified into a Tony Curtis, a style adopted by Elvis and based on that made fashionable by the movie star of the same name, in which the hair was grown long, swept back on both sides to meet in a line at the back of the head and held in place by copious applications of Brylcreem. The hair on the top of my head was curled over to form a sausage like construction. This style incorporated a feature known as a DA or 'ducks arse', because from the back it appeared like the tail of a duck, and was especially popular with Teddy Boys, a fact that made it unpopular with my mother. As a temporary alternative, I adopted a style of haircut popular with American servicemen, the crew cut, where the hair was cut very short and trained to stand vertically upwards on top of the head, like the stubble on a freshly mown field of corn. I quickly abandoned this style when I was advised by the barber that wearing a hairnet at night would help my hair to adopt the required vertical stance. I could not cope with the thought of wearing a hairnet. For a short time I managed to combine the two styles by replacing the sausage of the Tony Curtis by a small triangular area of crew cut on the top of my head. The adoption of special hairstyles by many young men resulted in hats becoming a thing of the past. My father always wore a hat, normally a flat cap, while my Grandfather Miller usually wore a trilby. I wore a cap to school until I was 14 but after that I went hatless, even in the wettest of weather.

During the 1950s, going to the cinema was one of the main forms of entertainment for most people. Before the arrival of our first television set, going to the pictures was a regular event, not only for me but also for my parents. Every town possessed at least one cinema or picture house to cater for this demand. In Great Yarmouth we had the luxury of five cinemas to choose from: the Regal, Regent, Aquarium, Empire and Windmill, more than most other towns of an equivalent size. Monthly film shows were also held in many local village halls and I regularly watched films with my friends at the halls in nearby Martham, Fleggburgh and Ormesby. My mother was a keen picture-goer and went to the cinema at least once a week. In the holidays, I frequently accompanied her on a weekday shopping trip to Great Yarmouth that normally included an afternoon at the cinema. In my middle teens I joined the gangs of young people who travelled every Sunday during the winter months on the afternoon bus from Rollesby and its neighbouring villages to Great Yarmouth for a film and a fish and chip supper before catching the 9.05pm last service bus back home. In my late teens, the cinema was the natural location for a first date with a girlfriend.

It was inevitable that the cinema would have a big influence on my musical development. My mother was particularly fond of musicals and with her I saw numerous song-and-dance films including *White Christmas*, *Singing in the Rain*, *Band Waggon*, *Seven Brides for Seven Brothers* and many movies from the '*Road*' series featuring Bing Crosby and Bob Hope, as well as numerous re-issues of Busby Berkeley and Fred Astaire and Ginger Rogers' productions. As most of these were made in America, I was greatly influenced by and enjoyed immensely the music from their sound tracks, especially American band music, including 1930s jazz and the big band sounds from the 1940s and 1950s. On my own, I preferred to watch war films and westerns, but even these often had musical dimensions. Along with many teenagers, I sang along to Jimmy Young's version of *The Man from Laramie* and Bill Hayes' composition *Davy Crockett, King of the Wild Frontier*, although I was never tempted to buy a Davy Crockett racoon hat.

Throughout my time in Leicester I continued to be an avid picture-goer, watching films on average once a week. I regularly travelled into the city centre to visit the ABC Savoy in Belgrave Gate, the Gaumont on the market, the Picture House on Granby Street and the Odeon on Rutland Street, and, occasionally, the more distant Trocadero, Roxy, Evington and Fosse cinemas; sometimes on my own but more often than not with a female companion or a noisy gang of students out for a good time. My favourite cinema in Leicester was the Cameo, a small establishment on the High Street that specialised in fringe and continental films, some of which often included a more explicit sexual content than was usual in British films of the time. The Cameo 'Electric Theatre', built in 1910, was allegedly the first purpose built cinema in Leicester. I spent many evenings on the back row of the Cameo with a girlfriend, occasionally watching the film. On one unforgettable evening, the lights came up at the end of the show to reveal that the occupant of the adjacent seat to me was a well-known university lecturer with his arm firmly stuck up the jumper of his female companion sitting next to him.

At 16, my preference at the cinema was for escapist adventure films: westerns, historical sagas, war stories and detective thrillers. Yet I also enjoyed romantic films, although I would never admit it to my friends. I drooled over Marilyn Monroe in *Some Like it Hot* and Debbie Reynolds in *Susan Slept Here*, and fantasised over Audrey Hepburn, Virginia Mayo and Jane Russell whenever they appeared on the screen. But by the early 1960s, my horizons had expanded to include films that highlighted the issues and inequalities that existed in contemporary society, particularly those issues that affected young people. I identified strongly with the topics highlighted in the British New Wave or 'kitchen sink' films. These films were usually adapted from the novels of many contemporary authors, especially those authors who had become labelled as 'angry young men' because their storylines attempted to depict the frustrations and dramas in the lives of ordinary working people in post-war Britain. Often the principal character was an alienated young man attempting to rebel against and break free from the social and economic deprivation of his working-class background. The first of these films that I saw was Karel Reisz's 1960 production of *Saturday Night and Sunday Morning* in which Albert Finney portrayed the disenchanted Arthur Seaton as he became confronted with the problems of sex, pregnancy, abortion and personal responsibilities. I was so taken with the film that I saw it twice on the same day. I empathised strongly with Rita Tushingham's character Jo in *A Taste of Honey*, a film that sympathetically addressed the issues of unmarried pregnancy, racial prejudice and homosexuality.

Among the many other films that I enjoyed were Alfred Hitchcock's psychological thrillers, including Cary Grant being pursued by secret agents in *North by North West* (1959), his strange and frightening story of *The Birds* (1963) and I was suitably horrified by the unexpected twists in the plot of *Psycho* (1960), especially when the main character in the story was brutally murdered in her shower halfway through the film. How audiences were persuaded not to reveal the nature of these twists after they had seen the film remains a complete mystery. I was also excited by the action adventures of Sean Connery in *Dr No* (1962), the first of his many appearances as Ian Fleming's charismatic spy James Bond, and the never-to-be-forgotten vision of Ursula Andress as Honey Ryder emerging from the sea clad only in a wet white bikini.

In my capacity as booking secretary for the Leicester University Film Society, I was required not only to book, receive and return films to an agency but also to produce a brief critique of each film that appeared on the programme at the Society's fortnightly meeting in the Queen's Hall. My critiques, typed onto A4 Banda paper and laboriously reproduced on a spirit duplicator, were hardly ever read, but were turned into paper aeroplanes by a rowdy audience and propelled into the projector beam amid cheers of delight as the shadow of a paper plane crossed over the screen. Often a film's dialogue was enhanced by an inappropriate loud comment from a member of the audience and every embrace on the screen was greeted with a raucous cheer from the gallery. Despite these juvenile antics, the film club widened my appreciation for the cinema in general and introduced me to many thought provoking classic and foreign-made films. I marvelled at the polished acting of Orson Wells in *Citizen Kane*, a story about the corrupting influence of money and power, as well as Swedish director Ingmar Bergman's sombre and dour productions of *The Seventh Seal* and *Wild Strawberries*. The futility of war was realistically portrayed in Andrzej Wajda's trilogy *A Generation*, *Kanal* and *Ashes and Diamonds*, set in World War Two Poland and Erich Maria Remarque's World War One epic *All Quiet on the Western Front*. I enjoyed especially Brazilian made *Orfeu Negro* (*Black Orpheus*) and Akira Kurosawa's exciting *Seven Samurai* (the original Japanese film that Hollywood remade as *The Magnificent Seven*), as well as numerous short experimental productions. Not that all of the films made any sense to me. I confidently discussed the social implications of the film *La Dolce Vita* with a group of Italian students at Brucciani's coffee bar on Horsefair Street, despite my extremely limited understanding of its content. Heaven only knows what they thought!

Fortnightly Film Club

Certain sections of the university seem to take a warped delight in annoying other sections of their fellow students. This is particularly in evidence during very good film shows arranged by the Film Society. At the showing of 'The Battleship Potemkin' on the 28th October, the ridiculous behaviour of some people in the gallery caused great annoyance to those generally interested in the nature and technique of the film. Are some students incapable of reading any interpretation, other than the bawdy and lewd, into basically good scripts and sound tracks? Perhaps they are emotionally immature; and an unconscious embarrassment at frank realism causes this reaction. In this respect we are thinking especially of those films which treat the sensual side of human relationships in an enlightened and intelligent manner.

Correspondence, *Ripple*, 6 November 1959

The success of *Rock Around the Clock* stimulated the production of numerous films that promoted the sound of rock 'n' roll. These films became essential viewing for most popular music fans. In most cases the story lines were weak and were clearly intended simply as a vehicle for popular beat music. The first film that I saw after *Rock Around the Clock* that featured a rock 'n' roll singer was *Love Me Tender*, starring Elvis Presley, which was shown at the Royal Aquarium cinema in Great Yarmouth during January 1957. My friend Richard and I were ardent fans of Elvis Presley and so we joined the long queue outside the cinema, expecting to be entertained by a film containing numerous songs sung by Elvis. However, the film was a great disappointment because it turned out to be an unexciting American Civil War drama that featured just one Elvis song, the slow ballad *Love Me Tender*. Our disappointment was shared by the multitude of young women who screamed every time Elvis appeared on the screen and tried unsuccessfully to dance rock 'n roll in the aisles to his singing. Nevertheless, the recording of *Love Me Tender* soon appeared at the top of the popular music charts.

The sequel to *Rock Around the Clock*, entitled *Don't Knock the Rock*, featured Bill Haley and his Comets, Alan Dale, Little Richard, The Treniers and Dave Appell and his Applejacks. It was equally as disappointing as *Love Me Tender*. Had it not been for the lively renditions of *Tutti-Frutti* and *Long Tall Sally* by a manic Little Richard, it would have done little to advance my appreciation for rock 'n' roll. Thankfully, my faith was restored by the release of two Elvis Presley films: *Jailhouse Rock*, later in 1957 and *King Creole* in 1958. The title songs for both of these films reached number 1 and number 2 respectively in the popular music charts of 1958. I watched the new British heart-throb, Cliff Richard, making an unconvincing appearance as an exploited singer in *Espresso Bongo* in 1959. Once Elvis Presley had completed his compulsory two years of service in the US Army, his films appeared to lose their rebellious nature and he gradually developed as a mainstream entertainer. The storylines of *GI Blues* (1960), *Blue Hawaii* (1961) and *Girls, Girls, Girls* (1962) failed to excite me. Even Cliff Richard lost his rebellious look and displayed a blander but more acceptable side to his character in *The Young Ones* (1961) and *Summer Holiday* (1963). The most lauded musical of the early 1960s was the 1961 release, *West Side Story*, although it was not really a rock 'n' roll film. A sense of excitement was restored with *A Hard Day's Night* (1964), the Beatles' first film, made in the manner of *Rock Around the Clock* in that had a weak storyline and was badly acted, although the musical content was terrific.

Although I regularly attended film shows during my youth, visits to the theatre were few and far between. Other than concert parties and Christmas pantomimes at local village halls, school productions, amateur dramatic and summertime variety shows in Great Yarmouth, I had little opportunity in my corner of Norfolk to experience a good quality professional production. Until the Phoenix Theatre opened in 1963, there was no professional theatre available in Leicester either. My first real opportunity to see a top class theatrical performance came when I signed up for a pre-Christmas coach trip to London, organised by the university's Mathematics Society in 1961. The visit included an afternoon's guided tour of Watney's Brewery, followed by the evening performance of Keith Waterhouse's *Billy Liar* at the Cambridge Theatre in London's West End, starring Tom Courtney as the compulsive liar, Billy Fisher. The trip was a most enjoyable experience as it was not only my first journey along the M1 motorway, but also my first tour of a brewery and my first visit to a West End theatre. As it happened, the hospitality at the brewery was so good that by the end of the tour many of our party were badly intoxicated and behaved in an embarrassingly rowdy manner during the performance of the play. Two were sick, while several others fell asleep. On the way back to Leicester, during a midnight rest stop at the newly-opened Watford Gap motorway service station on the M1, I was sufficiently recovered to treat myself to a very expensive but greasy traditional English breakfast, while some of my companions recovered in the toilet.

In 1964, Celia and I were taken to Stratford to see the newly formed Royal Shakespeare Company's production of *Henry IV, Part 1* directed by Peter Hall with Ian Porter as King Henry and Hugh Griffith as Falstaff. During the performance, I discovered to my delight that Shakespeare's plays are best seen on the stage and were not meant to be read from a book. Many opportunities existed at university for students to try their skills at acting, but I was never sufficiently confident or interested enough to participate. Celia made the best of her chances with the Players' Theatre at Trinity College in Dublin and the Inca's singer, Rod, appeared in many Leicester University productions, but I found the three lines that I was expected to deliver in the performance of *A Million Miles to the Moon* a daunting challenge that I did not wish to repeat.

Despite living independently for over two years in a student flat, I arrived at 40 Evington Street still ignorant of cooking. It was only when money was short and no alternative presented itself that desperation forced me to prepare my own meals, usually eggs, sausages and tomatoes cooked in the frying pan. Otherwise, the kitchen was unknown territory, with the exception of brewing coffee. Yet I was beginning to eat better than I had done in the past. The enhanced income that came from my various occupations was sufficient for me to be able to afford at least one bought meal a day. Providing that milk was available and nobody had raided the sparse provisions in my designated section of the kitchen cupboard, breakfast consisted of shredded wheat or Weetabix in cold milk before I departed for work at the hospital. During the week I bought a meal at lunchtime in the hospital canteen, usually a wholesome stodgy dish, high in carbohydrate but extremely filling: macaroni cheese, meat patty, stew, toad-in-the-hole, shepherd's pie, omelettes and salads, all usually served with a large helping of mashed potato or chips.

After group practice with the Mystics on Saturdays, I normally spent some time talking and socialising with the other members of the band. Rehearsals were great fun in Alan's tiny front room, in the course of which we provided a noisy entertainment for most of his long-suffering neighbours. The Saturday morning practice sessions were made even more delightful by Alan's mother, Mrs Makin, a dapper widow lady in her early 50s, who provided tea and cakes for all 'her boys'. Like a mother hen, she always insisted on making lunch for all of the band members as well, normally eggs, bacon, sausages and beans. Every Sunday, I joined many of my fellow flat-dwellers at the Blue Lagoon Restaurant, a small establishment on Waterloo Street near to the London Road Railway Station, which served relatively cheap meals. Every Sunday I dined on the Blue Lagoon's version of Venetian Steak. An unusual concoction of minced meat and herbs, closely resembling a large beef-burger, served with vegetables, chips and gravy. Evening meals were a rarity, not just for me but for all my other flatmates as well. We simply existed on coffee, cigarettes and alcohol during the evening, wherever we were.

On the few occasions that I had money to spend, I visited the local fish and chip shop for a portion of chips served in a newspaper. I hardly ever bought their fish because I found that it compared unfavourably with the fish sold on Great Yarmouth's market, which was not surprising because Leicester was located some distance from the nearest fishing port. Instead, I occasionally bought one of the shop's alternative takeout offerings: sausages in batter, meat pies or faggots. John's passion for pig's trotters was not shared by the rest of the household. No other takeaway meals were available in our area of Leicester. The Taj-Mahal Indian restaurant did not provide takeout curry meals and there were no pizza, burger or Chinese takeaway outlets in Highfields. The fashion for convenience foods and takeaway meals had yet to happen. Having heard of my experience behind the bar of the Old Horse public house, Reg Alexander, the new manager of the Percy Gee students' bar, occasionally employed me as a relief barman during weekday evenings. The fee might have been a pittance, but every evening that I was employed in the bar entitled me to two free pints of beer and a meal from the Percy Gee restaurant which, at the time, was more welcome than money.

Once Celia and I were engaged things became even better, because every Sunday thereafter I was invited to her parents' house for a roast dinner and every Wednesday for a steak meal, even when Celia was away in Dublin. Celia's home background was very similar to my own and so she naturally assumed the responsibility for organising our meals as soon as we were married, despite the fact that her culinary knowledge was limited. Her first purchase was a large brown earthenware stew pot in which most of our weekday meals were prepared and which, as she was a strict vegetarian, was normally a thick stew of vegetables and pulses; fortunately, with practice she soon became a competent cook. A brief attempt to provide me with meat-based meals ceased when she eventually refused to enter a butcher's shop, professing that the smell of blood made her feel sick. So after that, I became a vegetarian at home and a meat eater when we dined out. Not that dining out was easy. In the early 1960s, vegetarians were regarded as cranks and little effort was made by most restaurants to cater for their tastes. For Celia, eating out meant a diet of salads and omelettes. Even the ubiquitous vegetable lasagne had yet to appear on any restaurant menu. Only Indian cuisine offered an edible vegetarian meal for her to eat. Things changed slightly for the better with the opening of the Hungry-I Pancake House in 1962, an upstairs restaurant on the corner of Free Lane and Charles Street that served savoury and sweet pancakes, offering several vegetarian choices. Many lunchtimes and evenings were spent eating pancakes while being serenaded by jazz music from the Sonny Monk Quartet.

Of all the changes that took place during my stay in Leicester, the adoption of coffee in preference to tea was the most radical. I rarely drank coffee at all in Norfolk, but, as a student, coffee drinking was an almost continuous activity throughout the day. In the evenings, coffee and cigarettes acted as appetite suppressants and provided the energy to talk or study late into the night. During the day I spent most of my non-study time away from lectures talking and smoking with my friends in the coffee bar. The

Brucciani's Coffee bar on Horsefair Street was a regular Saturday morning destination for students. (by permission of the Record Office for Leicestershire, Leicester and Rutland)

The Chameleon Coffee House gave emerging folk and jazz entertainers an opportunity to display their talents. (R. Davies)

Percy Gee coffee bar did more than sell coffee; it was, in reality, a snack bar for drinks, sandwiches, rolls and light meals. A second serving hatch opened in the evening for the sale of alcohol. I met friends from the Art and Tech and the Scraptoft Training College for coffee at various venues around the city centre, including Brucciani's on Horsefair Street and the El Casa Bolero on Castle Street, allegedly Leicester's first specialist coffee bar. While Brucciani's was my favourite meeting place, it was not a conventional coffee bar, but first and foremost an ice-cream parlour and snack bar. By 1963 numerous other coffee bars had been established, including the Bar Roma on Charles Street and the very popular Chameleon on King Street. The Chameleon was a regular meeting place for young people, especially students, where we drank coffee while listening to jazz records or being serenaded by amateur folk singers

El Casa Bolero, allegedly the first coffee house in Leicester and a popular meeting place for beatniks, mods, rockers and students. (by permission of the Record Office for Leicestershire, Leicester and Rutland)

and, occasionally, we listened to a performance from a classical guitarist. Every Tuesday was folk night at the Chameleon.

I normally preferred the bar at the Percy Gee for an alcoholic drink in the evening, because not only was it the prime meeting place for students but it was also subsidised and very cheap. Not that I could afford to drink to excess because, for most of my undergraduate days, three drinks was my limit and then only at weekends or on special occasions. I normally chose to drink a mixture of a bottle of light ale and a half of bitter. Binge drinking was left primarily to the macho members of the rugby club. Their drinking games were legendary, particularly one that was called 'the boat race', and were normally accompanied by the singing of extremely rude songs. If I did venture out for a drink at a public house, I preferred to spend my time at the White Horse in Oadby or the Old Horse and the Marquis of Wellington, both on the London Road; premises that were popular with students because of their proximity to the university and the men's halls of residence. I also regularly visited the Victoria on Granby Street, the Dover Castle and the Red Cow on Belgrave Gate because of the folk song clubs that met in their upstairs function rooms or in the intimate atmosphere of their back room bars. Although I spent many evenings in public houses, I was rarely intoxicated as I preferred dancing, singing and meeting young women to excessive drinking. I quickly discovered that the two did not readily mix. My only adventure with excessive drinking and the first time that I experienced the confusing state of being 'legless', occurred when I was introduced to Celia's Uncle Bill at the White Swan in the Market Place. Bill was a working-class socialist intellectual and every Friday met with a group of similarly minded middle-aged men to discuss politics and literature, read poetry and drink vast quantities of alcohol. During the evening that I spent with him and his social group, my protestations that three drinks was my limit fell on deaf ears and, as a consequence, during the walk home to our flat my legs ceased to work and I was literally dragged along by an impatient Celia.

CHAPTER 16

ENTERTAINMENT IN THE HOME

For most of my student days money was short and, as a result, much of my leisure time was spent at home talking with my friends, drinking coffee, smoking, reading books, playing cards, singing and strumming my guitar. Deep meaningful conversations often continued well into the night when all the ills and inequalities of the world were discussed and possible solutions suggested and argued about in smoke-filled sitting rooms. Coffee cups and ash-trays lay scattered all over our floors. Everybody smoked as it was the drug of the time, despite the expense. When money was tight we bought cheap un-tipped cigarettes – Woodbines, Park Drive or Player's Weights – often cutting them in half with a razor blade to eke them out. For a while, I tried smoking a pipe and I often filled its bowl with cigarette ends from the ash-trays to satiate my need for nicotine.

Many at the university were concerned that they could sense a general deterioration in standards among students. Dress codes were certainly changing. By the time I started my second year, my cavalry twill and grey flannel trousers were often replaced by hard-wearing corduroy and blue denim jeans, my shirt and tie by a T-shirt and sweater, and my sports jacket by either a red, blue and black checked lumberjack's coat or a black donkey jacket. My suit was relegated to the wardrobe, only to be worn on very special occasions and for interviews. Some male students continued wearing suits, sports jackets, shirts and ties every day, but they were rapidly becoming a minority. As was the case with many of my student colleagues, it was a lack of money rather than slovenliness that had dictated my preference for cheaper and more hard-wearing clothes, although this fact was not always appreciated by others.

> A well-pressed suit worn with dignity can be the indication of a gentleman and is surely not beyond anyone's means. Please do not, for the sake of your own pride, continue to ask us girls to stomach the untidy, too often unwashed and altogether slovenly (even if they are angry) young men we are so often encountering in the Common Room and Coffee Bar.
>
> Correspondence, *Ripple*, 6 February 1960

In the provinces, the pressure on young people to follow the latest fashions in clothing was not as great as it was in London. Only a small minority felt the need to dress every day in the latest style. For most young people, not just students, fashionable clothes were far too expensive. My wardrobe normally consisted of a set of work clothes, a small selection of casual wear and a best suit. Like me, my father's work clothes consisted of redundant every day wear, in his case a pair of grey trousers, a white shirt, a tie, a sleeveless pullover and a jacket, all covered by a blue overall and topped with a flat cap. Even my mother donned a garishly patterned housecoat when working at home. At school, my working dress was my school uniform but at university I attended lectures in my older casual wear. The notion of a uniform for students was abandoned when the student body voted not to wear gowns for lectures. My everyday casual wear followed the current trends of the time, but was hardly the height of fashion. Blue denim jeans became my trousers of choice. New jeans were often worn while I sat in the bath in an attempt to fade the colour and to shrink them so that they might fit snuggly. Brown corduroy trousers with narrow bottoms were an occasional alternative. As jeans were usually sold in just one fit-all leg size, my jeans were frequently worn with large turn-ups at the bottom of each leg despite the fact that turn-ups were regarded as old fashioned.

The rest of my clothes were quite conventional. I usually wore a plain T-shirt and a sweater under by my lumberjack's coat or my donkey jacket. On my feet, I wore suede shoes, long desert boots or my favourite brown elastic sided ankle length Chelsea boots. My attempt to follow the current fashions in clothing was achieved simply by adding small touches to my everyday dress because I could not afford to buy the latest fashionable outfits that were on sale in Leicester's city centre. When I wore a shirt, I preferred to wear ones that were colourful rather than plain white. My favourite shirt had wide red, grey and black vertical stripes, which I usually wore with a narrow black leather tie. I replaced my old-fashioned underwear by T-shirts and Y-front pants. A few of my more fortunate student colleagues were keen followers of fashion. Many were influenced by the growing popularity for Italian or French style clothing and were often dressed in smart suits with short jackets, round collared shirts, narrow trousers with no turn-ups, Parka overcoats with fur-trimmed hoods and winkle-picker shoes. I too was persuaded to buy two pairs of winkle-picker shoes – a light tan pair fastened by a buckle and a pair of black cowboy-style ankle length boots. Both were very cheap and, in no time at all, the long toe ends began to turn upwards so that they quickly resembled the style of footwear worn by a mediaeval minstrel.

By 1964, the fashion styles of the Mods and the Rockers were becoming apparent in the Percy Gee. Mods and Rockers were two very different rival sub-groups within British youth culture of the early 1960s. Rockers were primarily working-class young men and women who preferred to follow the rock 'n' roll culture of the late 1950s, especially the music of Elvis Presley, Gene Vincent and the late Eddie Cochran. Imitating the rebellious characters portrayed by Marlon Brando and James Dean at the cinema, they wore leather jackets, blue jeans and boots and, if they could afford it, they rode motorcycles. Mods were mainly from middle-class backgrounds, dressed Italian style and rode Vespa or Lambretta scooters. Those students who followed the current fashionable trends usually favoured the fashion styles of the Mods, although most male students continued to remain conservative in their choice of dress.

Women were certainly more fashion conscious than men. The flared skirts popular in the late 1950s were gradually replaced by slim black skirts and white blouses. Suits consisting of a jacket and skirt were often adopted as smart casual wear. Celia married in a suit in preference to a wedding dress, because a suit could be worn afterwards for special occasions. A wedding dress was considered an unnecessary expense when money was tight. Wearing trousers was also becoming popular with women. Ankle length slacks with zips up the side and woollen black tights worn with long baggy sweaters were common. At the time, my mother hated women in trousers but, eventually, began wearing them herself. But the most obvious fashion change was in hairstyles. Celia's short hairstyle was soon replaced by a longer bouncy backcombed style, the most elaborate version of which was called the 'beehive'. My hairstyle was little changed although I had ceased plastering my hair with Brylcreem and began combing the top forward in the style of the Beatles' Mop, mainly to cover up my receding hairline. Again, influenced by the fashions of the jazz fans, I grew a small goatee beard.

Where reading was concerned, my preference for non-fiction meant that my knowledge of popular literature was extremely limited. Until 1963, what knowledge I had was derived almost exclusively from the cinema and not from books. As a child, I had read most of the standard classics including *Treasure Island*, *Lorna Doone*, *Black Beauty*, *Great Expectations* and *David Copperfield* but little else. Celia, on the other hand, had an insatiable appetite for literature and read three or four books of fiction every week. Once we were married, she introduced me to popular literature and we systematically worked our way through many literary genre including selected novels from the authors of Kitchen Sink, detective, science fiction and spy stories. Through my reading I became familiar with the detective prowess of Albert Campion, Father Brown, Lord Peter Wimsey, Mike Hammer, Philip Marlowe and the Saint. I enjoyed the imaginative science fiction of *Caves of Steel* by Isaac Asimov, *The Time Machine* by H.G. Wells, *The Sands of Mars* by Arthur C. Clarke, Kurt Vonnegut's *Sirens of Mars* and John

Wyndham's *Day of the Triffids*. I was enthralled by *Our Man in Havana*, *The Ipcress File*, *The 39 Steps* and Ian Fleming's James Bond spy thrillers, but my favourites of all the books that I read were astronomer Fred Hoyle's novel *The Black Cloud* and the suspense story *Watcher in the Shadows* by Geoffrey Household, the first for its thoughtful content and the second for its tense and gripping story-line. Books that we bought were passed around among our friends or swapped for a different title; others were borrowed from various libraries.

Many evenings we played card games of one kind or another. It was a skill that most young people developed during the 1950s and '60s. I cannot remember when I first began to play cards. By the age of 13 I played Gin Rummy and Cribbage with my father and was confident and competent enough at Whist to join my parents and grandparents at village Whist drives. Playing regularly with my family quickly gave me the ability to play all forms of competitive Whist, including German and Contract Whist. Inevitably, at grammar school I was introduced to gambling games, in particular Pontoon, three card Brag and Poker. Often at weekends six or more of my sixth-form colleagues gathered at a designated venue to spend a long night gambling at cards and drinking beer. Not that we were serious gamblers or drinkers because our finances were very limited. Half-penny stakes were the norm and a large bottle of Lacon's Pale Ale each would last most of an evening.

At university I was introduced to Contract Bridge. Both my roommates in Beaumont Hall were Bridge players and very soon our room became the venue for many late night Bridge rubbers. Before university I had never played Bridge. It was considered by most of my family to be a game for the middle classes and not for working people. In 1959, as Leicester University was still very much a middle-class dominated establishment, playing Bridge was normal. From the moment that it opened in the morning until it closed last thing at night, there was always a Bridge game in progress at the JCR in the Percy Gee, the players often surrounded by a dozen or more knowledgeable spectators. Bridge was considered a serious business for some students because some games were played for money. It was inadvisable for any inexperienced Bridge player to join a game played for money as the stakes, based on the points scored, were often very high. Poker games were also common throughout the day. A few hardened students, expert in the art of bluff and double bluff, purposefully added to their grant in fiercely contested poker games. Many new first year students quickly learned that there were no friends to be made in love, war or in games of Poker and Bridge. My friends and I mostly played Hearts, a game for four or more players sometimes known as Black Queen or Dirty Lady. When Celia was ill, Roy and Liz often joined us on her bed for long games of Hearts. When Celia and I were alone, we played against each other in highly competitive games of Bezique.

Very often our small flats were filled with the sound of music. When Celia moved to Evington Street she brought with her a Dansette record player with an automatic record changing mechanism and her collection of records, including songs recorded by the Everly Brothers, Roy Orbison, Ricky Nelson, Adam Faith and Cliff Richard. Once married, we added to her collection with purchases of long-playing records, mostly by the Beatles – *Please, Please Me* (1963), *With the Beatles* (1963), *A Hard Day's Night* (1964) and *Beatles for Sale* (1964) – as well as a few singles including our favourite recording of *House of the Rising Sun* by Eric Burdon and the Animals.

During my student days at Leicester, access to a radio was limited. At Beaumont Hall, radio sets and record players were allowed only to the residents of single rooms. However, a very busy social life ensured that I spent little time listening to the wireless. The only access to a radio for those in a shared occupation was via a rarely used radiogram located in a small back room of the main Beaumont Hall building. My flat at East Park Road was equipped with a large old-fashioned valve radio of indeterminate age which John and I often used to listen to jazz and popular music programmes, while at Gopsall and Evington Streets I relied on radios supplied by my flatmates. My personal radio in my bedroom at home in Norfolk was too bulky to transport to Leicester and so I had no wireless of my own until I bought the small silver and blue battery-powered transistor radio as a gift for Celia on our wedding day. This neat and eminently portable radio not only provided non-stop background entertainment for Celia and me but also enlivened our walks in the park and long train journeys to Norfolk, much to the annoyance of our fellow travellers. Whenever possible we listened in the evenings to programmes from Radio Luxembourg. But by the early 1960s, the BBC had reacted to the popularity of Radio Luxembourg by transmitting many popular music programmes of their own, which also became essential listening, including Brian Matthew's *Saturday Club* and *Easy Beat* (the former a spin-off from BBC's *Saturday Skiffle Club*), as well as *Pick of the Pops* introduced by David Jacobs. In March 1964, we were excited when we managed to receive the first transmissions from *Radio Caroline*, a ship-based pirate radio station in the style of Radio Luxembourg that played popular music all day and every day.

Other than during vacations or on my occasional term-time hitchhiking trips home to Rollesby, my time at university was also television free. In 1959, there were no television sets in evidence at Beaumont Hall or at the main university site. Not that this mattered as I was fully occupied with academic studies, learning how to look after myself away from my mother's tender care and exploring to excess the abundant temptations to be found in a student's leisure-time environment. A television set was occasionally placed in the JCR for students to use for special events. I joined many of my friends in the JCR to watch the FA Cup Finals of 1961 and 1963 because Leicester City (the Foxes) was one of the finalists. Despite raucous support from the students in the JCR, Leicester City's football team lost both of these matches: 2–0 to Tottenham Hotspurs in 1961 and 3–1 to Manchester United in 1963. By the summer of 1963, a television room had been established on the top floor of the Percy Gee where I joined many of my friends to watch England's cricket team play the West Indies. The second test match was memorable for the fact that we watched in awe as Colin Cowdrey batted with a broken arm and helped England to achieve a most creditable draw.

Television sets in flats were also a rarity as they were far too expensive for students on a grant. Only once was a television installed in any of the flats where I lived and then only for a very short time. When John re-joined our student community at 40 Evington Street, he brought with him an old battered black and white television set that was well past its use-by date Every week for the month or two that the set continued to function, a dozen or more students gathered in our cigarette smoke-filled lounge to drink coffee and watch the controversial satirical programme *That Was The Week That Was* (TW3) hosted by a young David Frost and to guffaw at the often politically and socially sensitive sketches that made up most of the programme's content. The television was hardly ever used for any other viewing as we had no licence and were in constant fear of being discovered by the detector vans that were allegedly touring around our neighbourhood.

On my return visits to Rollesby, I watched television constantly because my parents rarely switched their set off if there was a programme being broadcast. When independent Anglia Television began broadcasting in 1959, it allowed for a more varied choice of programmes, many of which were aimed at younger viewers. Television did much to promote popular music and I greatly enjoyed those programmes that I was able to see. Even before my introduction to rock 'n' roll, jazz and skiffle through the BBC's *6–5 Special* (1957–59), popular music had been screened on television in various programmes for the young, including BBC's *Hit Parade* (1952) and *Off the Record* (1955), the latter introduced by bandleader Jack Payne, as well as Independent Television's *TV Music Shop* (1955) with Pearl Carr and Teddy Johnson, and Kent Walton's *Cool for Cats* (1956–61). BBC replaced *6–5 Special* in January 1959 with *Dig This* (1959) featuring Bob Miller and his Millermen as the resident band, followed in April of the same year by the short-lived *Drumbeat* (1959), a programme that nevertheless launched the career of Adam Faith. This was also replaced in June 1959 by the rather sedate and un-teenage-like *Juke Box Jury* (1959–67), a programme hosted by David Jacobs in which invited guests judged the commercial potential of new record releases. BBC's most influential popular music series, *Top of the Pops* (1964–2006), was first screened on New Year's Day 1964 with a star-filled programme that featured the Beatles, the Rolling Stones, Dusty Springfield and the Hollies. Having left the *6–5 Special* to work for ITV, Jack Good produced the very successful programme *Oh Boy!* (1958–59), which was a popular music show that helped greatly to accelerate the musical career of Cliff Richard and the Shadows. This was followed by *Boy Meets Girl* (1959–60), featuring Marty Wilde, and, finally, *Wham* (1960). ITV's main alternative to *Top of the Pops* was *Ready, Steady, Go* (1963–66) introduced by Keith Fordyce and the charismatic Cathy McGowan.

Even after we were married, Celia and I did not own a personal television set until June 1964, when we were given a second-hand black and white set by her parents. The television set arrived on the same day that I was away in Norwich attending an interview for my first teaching post. On my return, I had to wait patiently until the end of an episode of *Dr Kildare* before I was allowed to tell Celia the good news of my appointment as a lecturer in mathematics at the Norwich City College of Further Education. After that we too became television addicts and most evenings were spent at home alone watching TV. From then onwards dancing and visiting the cinema were no longer our main forms of entertainment.

CHAPTER 17

CHANGING TASTES IN POPULAR MUSIC

My spare time was dominated by music: listening to music, playing music and dancing to music. Our identity was often defined by our choice of music. It became apparent to me that British skiffle and rock 'n' roll had lost their way by the early 1960s and had become staid and respectable. The British rock 'n' roll scene was dominated at that time by the Larry Parnes' Stable, a group of young British singers managed by impresario Larry Parnes, who performed under distinctive stage names such as Tommy Steele, Marty Wilde, Vince Eager, Billy Fury, Terry Dene, Dickie Pride, Johnny Gentle and Joe Brown – Joe Brown sensibly refused Parnes' suggestion that he should adopt the stage name of Elmer Twitch. I enjoyed many of their songs but not their stage images, because they were promoted as sanitised rock 'n' rollers – clean cut and neatly groomed all-round entertainers designed to appeal to every member of the family, from a teenager to a granny. It was not the rebellious image that I had come to expect from my rock 'n' roll heroes. I saw many of these performers when they appeared as summer season entertainers during the early 1960s in Parnes' Big Star Shows at Great Yarmouth. Billy Fury appeared at the Britannia Pier in 1960; Tommy Steele and Frankie Howard at the Windmill Theatre in 1961; Billy Fury, the Tornados, Marty Wilde and comedians Chic Murray and Maisie at the Windmill in 1962. Many of Parnes' stable also featured in Jack Goode's *Idols on Parade* at the De Montfort Hall in Leicester. Parnes' greatest success was with Tommy Steele who, under his guidance, progressed from his origins as a competent skiffle singer to become a world-class middle-of-the-road entertainer, completing his rise to fame by appearing and acting on stage in the musical *Half a Sixpence* at London's Cambridge Theatre in 1963. I enjoyed his 1956 versions of *Singing the Blues* and *Rock with the Cavemen*, but his later recordings of *Little White Bull* (1959), *What a Mouth* (1960) and *Flash Bang Wallop* (1963) did not have the same appeal.

At university, my interest in rock 'n' roll focussed primarily on the music of the Everly Brothers and Cliff Richard and the Shadows, together with a few odd recordings that took my fancy. I much preferred the more upbeat music of the late 1950s, as recorded by Lonnie Donegan, Buddy Holly, Elvis Presley and Eddie Cochran, to that offered by the British singers of the early 1960s, all eminently playable on an acoustic guitar. By 1963 popular music was dominated by the 'Mersey beat' and popular affection was transferred from Cliff Richard, the members of the Parnes' Stable and their ilk to the new, exciting

***Hello Dolly* was a hit for Louis Armstrong.**

and original Liverpool-based groups such as the Beatles, Jerry and the Pacemakers, the Swinging Blue Jeans and Billy J. Kramer and the Dakotas. The early 1960s was also the heyday for traditional jazz and jazz was my preferred listening both at home, at the university and about town. Jazz featured strongly in the top 20 music charts between 1959 and 1964, mainly recordings by Chris Barber, Acker Bilk, Kenny Ball and the Temperance Seven; Dinah Washington and Cleo Lane also had hit records during this period,

while Dave Brubeck's *Take Five* demonstrated that even modern jazz could be popular. *You're Driving Me Crazy* by the Temperance Seven reached number one in the music charts in May 1961 and Acker Bilk's recording of *Stranger on the Shore* topped the charts in January 1962. Even after its heyday was over, jazz continued to be popular with some sections of the public, particularly university and college students, but it never again achieved the heights it had enjoyed between 1959 and 1964, although Louis Armstrong had a belated hit record with *Hello Dolly* in 1964.

As traditional jazz started to wane in popularity, many jazz fans turned their attention towards Rhythm and Blues (R&B), as an alternative to the popular beat music of the day. Following visits to Britain by various American blues artists in the late 1950s (stars that included my old favourites Big Bill Broonzy, Muddy Waters, Sony Terry and Brownie McGhee), Chris Barber introduced an R&B spot into most of his gigs despite the fact that many jazz fans objected to this form of music, because it involved the frequent use of amplified guitars. These sessions gave birth to a number of London-based artists who promoted the raw and earthy sound of R&B as an alternative to the smoother and more sophisticated melodies of Cliff Richard and the later Beatles-led Liverpool sound. The most successful of the London R&B bands were Alexis Corner and his Blues Incorporated at the Marquee, Georgie Fame and the Blueflames at the Flamingo on Wardour Street, Long John Baldry, Cyril Davies and his All-Stars and, the best known of all, Mick Jagger and the Rolling Stones. While rock 'n' roll and R&B had much in common musically, most R&B bands presented themselves on stage in an informal, unkempt and generally disrespectful manner, which appealed greatly to the rebellious natures of some sections in their audiences.

As well as rock 'n' roll, jazz and R&B, many young people were developing an interest in folk music. When Rollesby Primary School acquired a radio for use during lessons, we listened every week to programmes for schools that encouraged pupils to sing and dance to traditional British folk songs. Along with the rest of my class I sang out-of-tune versions of *Bobby Shaftoe*, *Hearts of Oak*, *Barbara Allen* and *The British Grenadier* with enthusiasm and gusto. But for most teenagers of the 1950s, any interest they had in folk music began with skiffle because much of its musical content was adapted from traditional American and British folk songs – Lonnie Donegan's versions of *Cumberland Gap*, *The Battle of New Orleans* and *Bring a Little Water Sylvie,* Nancy Whiskey's *Freight Train* and the Kingston Trio's adaptation of *Tom Dooley*.

As the skiffle craze began to subside towards the end of the 1950s, like many young acoustic guitarists I began playing folk music because it provided me with the opportunity to play as an individual rather than requiring me to join a band or a group, as was the case for jazz and rock 'n' roll. The simplicity of many folk songs made them easy to sing and play for an inexperienced performer like myself. As a result, my musical repertoire included numerous traditional folk songs including *Scarborough Fair*, *The Gypsy Rover* and my mother's favourite, *Scarlet Ribbons*, as well as many rock 'n' roll, skiffle and American blues numbers. My links to Dave Cousins and the university's Folk Song Society ensured that my repertoire continued to expand and my playing expertise with an acoustic guitar continued to improve.

By the end of 1964, the term 'folk music' covered a broad spectrum of performing styles. For the purist minority, folk music was simply the songs of the ordinary labouring classes: traditional sea shanties, ballads and work songs occasionally performed by one or more individuals often without instrumental accompaniment, a musical style that appealed greatly to those of the political left because of its working-class origin. But folk music had also evolved to include upbeat modernised versions of traditional British or American folk songs played by a group or a band, often with amplified instruments, as illustrated by the music of Peter, Paul and Mary and the Springfields; and modern compositions arranged to sound like a traditional folk song, such as Marianne Faithfull's *As Tears Go By*. Also classified as folk music were the emerging new wave protest songs from the likes of Bob Dylan and Joan Baez.

Despite my involvement with jazz and folk music, from 1962 my performances with both the Incas and the Mystics ensured that my main musical development was in rock 'n' roll. By early 1963, Johnny Angel and the Mystics had turned into a very effective rock 'n' roll band and were beginning to obtain regular bookings, mainly in local clubs and dance halls. Through Ron's efforts, the Mystics were gaining in popularity especially in Leicester's many working men's clubs. We were regularly booked to play as one of the acts in each of the club's weekly variety shows, where we performed to a seated audience, often sandwiched between a comedian, a talent contest, bingo sessions and a stripper.

Inevitably, it became more and more difficult to play for both the Incas at the university and the Mystics in town, and I was forced to make a choice. In the end I elected to continue with the Mystics simply because the income I received from their performances was greater than that which I obtained from playing with the Incas. Every time I appeared with the Mystics, I was paid the princely sum of £1, an important consideration at a time when the lack of money was a matter for concern. My last appearance with the Incas was at the 1963 RAG Rave in Ulverscoft Drill Hall on Thursday 7 March, where we played on the same bill as the Farinas and the Johnny Hodgkins Hot Six jazz band featuring my old flatmate John from East Park Road days on trumpet. At the time, John was also living at 40 Evington Street, having replaced our artist in the attic accommodation. John's Hot Six was probably the best jazz band at that time in Leicester and included a blonde lady singer who allegedly once sang with the nationally known Alex Welsh Jazz Band, and banjo player, Phil Ward, recently returned from a tour of Germany with Long John Baldry and the Ken Sims Band. The Farinas were becoming well-known outside of Leicester and had begun touring around the country as

a supporting group at concerts headed by various top rock 'n' roll stars. The Farinas and the Hot Six took turns playing in the main hall while the Incas provided an alternative side-attraction in the smaller facility of the rifle range. For most of the evening, the range was packed so tightly with our supporters that dancing was impossible and most of the students merely listened to our music while sitting on the floor. Perhaps energised by their support, we played rock 'n roll as never before and our audience continually demanded encores. By the end of the evening, my fingers were sore,

Leicester University and Colleges

RAG RAVE

ULVERSCROFT ROAD DRILL HALL

THURSDAY MARCH 7th   8 - 12.30

Johnny Hodgkins Hot Six
The Incas Rock Group
The Farinas Rock Group

Licensed Bar   3/6

My last appearance with the Incas.

Charlie, Russ, Dave and me; the Incas reformed, dressed all in black with yellow braces; January 1963.

blistered and bleeding. Despite this apparent enthusiasm, not every student was a convert to rock 'n' roll. After I had left the Incas, Russ, Dave and Charlie continued to perform as a trio at society parties and Saturday dances until all three graduated and the Incas were finally disbanded.

After the Rag

Meanwhile, further junketings and jivings were going on at Ulverscroft Drill Hall, where 800 hot and sweaty students crammed themselves into a hot sweaty hall to listen and dance to the blatant cacophony of the most unmusical of musical groups imaginable. Everyone was, thankfully, in the later stages of stupefaction so no one noticed and consequently everyone enjoyed themselves.

Ripple, 22 March 1963

The gradual change in students' musical tastes was also evident at the many formal dances held throughout the university's academic year. As well as the Saturday Hop, popular well-attended dances were held during RAG Week in March and the more formal Christmas, Union and Summer Balls in December, February and June respectively. Dances held during RAG Week were joint ventures organised by the university and Leicester's many colleges, and were normally located at venues within the city that were capable of accommodating the large number of students attending each function. Four dances were held during the riotous seven days of the 1961 RAG Week: a Jazz Band Ball at the Palais de Danse on Humberstone Gate, a Rag Ball at the De Montfort Hall, Beat the Wheat at the Corn Exchange and a Grand Carnival Dance, also at the Palais. Music for these dances was usually provided by local Leicester-based groups except for the Rag Ball for which a nationally known band was normally engaged. The headline attraction at the Rag Ball in 1961 was Bob Miller and his Millermen, a well-known big band from TVs *Dig This* that was capable of providing music for ballroom dancing as well as rock 'n' roll and jive, with additional music provided by local jazz bands and rock groups. None of these dances, including the Rag Ball, were formal affairs and suits and ball-gowns were not a requirement. Students frequently attended in casual wear or fancy dress. As an undergraduate with a love of dancing, the RAG Week dances were a must. The cost of attending all these dances was so great that my tickets were frequently bought at the expense of food.

Bob Miller and his Millermen at the Rag Ball

It was felt by the (RAG) Committee that one of the country's outstanding strict tempo bands would make a welcome departure from the 'jiving only' policy of previous committees. Bob can play music with a 'beat' and at the same time is able to render a slow waltz as well as any other band in the country.

Ripple, 1 March 1961

The three university balls, however, were formal affairs and male students were expected to wear suits and the women dresses or ball-gowns. Music for dancing was usually provided by three bands: a traditional orchestra providing music for ballroom dancing, a jazz band for jiving and a novelty group. From 1959 until 1962, music for ballroom dancing was provided by the Danny Rogers' Orchestra but in 1963, following their earlier success at the Rag Ball, the choice was for the more upbeat and popular music of Bob Miller and his Millermen. Jazz music for jiving was provided at various times by Alex Welsh and his Dixielanders, Terry Lightfoot and his New Orleans Jazz Band, the Temperance Seven, Acker Bilk and his Paramount Jazz Band, the Original Dixieland Jazz Band (ODJB) and Kenny Ball. Novelty bands included the Malcolm Robmear Trio, a 'palm court' ensemble; South American music from the Cubanaires and Caribbean sounds from the Sparrow West Indian Steel Band. In 1962, Aztec and the Incas were invited to play rock 'n' roll. By 1964 all pretence at ballroom dancing had vanished

Trevor, Rod, me and friends at the 1961 Jazz Band Ball. The dress code was definitely informal during RAG Week. (R. Davies)

and entertainment was provided exclusively by popular rock groups. Brian Poole and the Tremeloes, the Pretty Things and the Farinas were the main bands at the 1964 Union Ball. Brian Poole and his band impressed me greatly with a most professional performance, one number following straight on from another for the duration of their set, including perfect live versions of their hit recordings *Twist and Shout*, *Do You Love Me* and *Candy Man*. On the other hand, the Pretty Things were neither pretty nor inspiring with their unimpressive interpretation of traditional R&B.

All the changes that were taking place within popular music were manifested in the evolving beat scene at Leicester, both at the university and in the city. In 1959 the weekly Saturday hop at the university was a traditional dance with an orchestra playing music for ballroom dancing; rock 'n' roll and jive were limited to short sessions where students danced to records or a guest group while the orchestra took a break. But by 1962 the rock 'n roll sessions had become longer, especially after the formation of the Incas. In a move to counter the drop in attendance at the hops they were eventually devoted entirely to a combination of jazz and rock 'n' roll. As jazz became less popular, rock 'n' roll became the dominant sound on a Saturday night; a trend that was not welcomed by some of the more traditionally minded university students.

After last term's taste of honey, i.e. the appearance of Fat John's Jazzmen at a hop, I had hoped that the Entertainments Committee had had a revelation. However this does not seem to be true, since I now understand that we are embarking on a 'Rock at the hop' campaign. Apart from having to suffer two lunchtime rock sessions and the indignation of hearing Rock on 'Jazznite', I had hoped that we might have heard jazz on Saturdays. But if we HAVE to twitch every Saturday then let the morons meet the intelligent half way with a Rhythm and Blues group.

Letters, *Ripple*, 7 February 1964.

In January 1964, the Entertainments Committee introduced the occasional Saturday Specials, which featured nationally known rock bands. The first of these Saturday Specials starred Peter Jay and the Jaywalkers with Frank Kelly and the Hunters, followed soon after by the Applejacks and, on Saturday 23 May, the Rolling Stones. The appearance of the Rolling Stones caused some consternation at the university and, fearing an invasion of fans from the city, the dance was made ticket only and security was intensified. The Percy Gee was shut at 4.30 in the afternoon and re-opened at 7.00 when nobody without a ticket was allowed onto the premises. A large police presence reflected the genuine concern among both the organisers and the local police force that fans who had been unable to obtain tickets might attempt to gatecrash the event, a concern that was fortunately unfounded. As my ex-flatmate Roy was a member of the Entertainments Committee, both Celia and I were treated favourably and had no difficulty in gaining entry to the gig. Trevor missed his opportunity but overcame the misfortune of being ticketless by locking himself and his girlfriend inside a convenient storeroom in the Percy Gee before it was shut at 3.30 in the afternoon. They re-emerged bleary eyed as soon as the building was re-opened at 7.00. Neither of them would say how they spent the intervening three and a half hours while locked in the storeroom. In many ways the evening was a disappointment because the Rolling Stones were either very drunk or under the influence of something stronger. As a result, their music was rough, raucous and very loud, while their behaviour verged on the obscene. Nevertheless, we danced until we were nearly exhausted.

Hop of the year

The Stones in reality weren't quite as ugly as one expected, and the sound they made was not refreshingly new. Their attitude of 'we're the Stones – so bugger you lot' didn't exactly win them new fans, but after the first half hour, it became obvious why they were so popular. The music became louder and more insistent, and Mick Jagger became more flaunty and seductive. At this point, they even seemed to be enjoying themselves and at the end neither they nor the audience wanted to go.

Ripple, 18 June 1964

By 1964, rock 'n' roll was definitely replacing jazz in the affections of Leicester's university students. Until then, jazz had dominated the university's beat music scene. Jazz was extensively covered by articles and reports in *Ripple* while rock 'n' roll and folk music were generally ignored or denigrated. Nevertheless, the Friday night jazz sessions at the Cellar Club continued to be a popular attraction until the cellar was closed down in 1963 when it was discovered that it contravened fire regulations because it had only one exit. The club continued for a short time in the JCR until that too was stopped because the JCR was not licensed for dancing. From 1961, an alternative attraction appeared in the guise of the Leicester University Jazz Club, which, for a while, organised lunchtime record sessions and live jazz concerts in the Queen's Hall. In 1962, the club persuaded the Universities' Jazz Federation to hold its regional semi-finals at the university on 21 February. Inca's Eric displayed his versatility by playing drums in Leicester University's entry into the competition. Despite its growing popularity, rock 'n' roll, with its working-class image, was not readily accepted by some of Leicester's middle-class students and many of them expressed their disapproval openly, especially once lunchtime rock 'n' roll dance sessions were a regular feature in the Percy Gee.

Depravity

As a sociologist in my second year and intensely interested in the fine and graceful art of ballroom dancing, I decided last Thursday to visit the Large Music Room where, every Tuesday and Thursday, for the meagre sum of 6d, unlimited quantities of 'Rock' can be heard. I was genuinely astonished, nay even shocked, when I entered. Was I in Leicester University or some weird figment of a junkie's imagination? Males and females pranced, cavorted, stamped and swayed before my eyes, kicking sideways with their feet or making strange obscene gestures with their mouths and hands whilst the record player blared forth its hideous row drowning all conversation and thought. After a few minutes I fled, horrified, away from the terrible scene. I knew this kind of dancing as depravity of the lowest order and as a member of the Christian

Union I earnestly hope that these potential orgies will be discontinued in the very near future.

Letters, *Ripple*, 24 October 1963.

Parallel with rock 'n' roll's growth in popularity at the university, came an apparent deterioration in student behaviour that was often ascribed to the growing numbers of working-class students who were entering into higher education. Whether it was true or not, behaviour certainly became more outrageous during the early 1960s. By 1963, drunkenness and loutish behaviour had begun to deter the more sensitive among the student population from using the Percy Gee at weekends. It was the sort of behaviour that caused *Ripple* correspondents to suggest that the Union was under the influence of 'Yobocracy'. Attendance at the weekly Saturday Hops dropped alarmingly and, without remedial action, they were in great danger of being cancelled indefinitely. The 1964 RAG week was notorious for the unacceptable behaviour of some students. Many of the RAG Week stunts became audacious in the extreme, despite the creation of a disciplinary committee to clamp down on student misbehaviour. Students occupying Leicester's historic Newark Gateway threw missiles and flour bombs at members of the police force who were trying to remove them from the premises, while another group managed to stop a Leicester to London express train by pulling the emergency cord while one student feigned a heart attack. The RAG Rave at the Granby Halls, which was attended by over 6,000 party-goers and featured Gene Vincent, the Merseybeats and the Farinas, degenerated into confusion when fights broke out between drunken students and groups of equally inebriated local Leicester youths.

> The entertainment was good, but the foulness of the place tended to make the fact that the music was good very secondary. Bottle fights were frequent, many girls fainted, and a mass strip was seen to be taking place by the stage where the Merseybeats were playing. There was nothing about the function to indicate that here was the introduction to gay, swinging Rag Week.
>
> *Ripple*, 12 March 1964.

For me, the 1964 RAG Rave was the beginning of the end, because it was the night when I suddenly realised that I was no longer one of the young ones. That mantle had passed to a new generation of students who, in their turn, were challenging the boundaries of behaviour created by the generation of students that had preceded them. While I greatly enjoyed the music and the dance, I was uncomfortable with some elements of what I saw around me, especially the drunkenness and the violence that took

The Newark Gateway was the location for many student disturbances during the notorious 1964 RAG week.

place in a thick fog of cigarette and cannabis smoke. I had seen extreme drunkenness before but had regarded it as a masculine trait, a rite of passage that should be experienced at least once by every adolescent male. I had always regarded women as being the more sensible sex, but in the Granby Halls I saw young women as insensible as the males that they accompanied, often lying on the floor entwined around each other. I was also well used to seeing couples in a passionate embrace, but I must admit to being a little bit shocked when I realised that some of those couples were of the same sex.

Not only had ballroom dancing become a thing of the past but rock 'n' roll dancing was rapidly heading down the same road. Conventional dance bands were rarely seen at university dances and few students knew how to dance the foxtrot or the quickstep. The last waltz had been replaced by an undignified shuffle in which the lady draped her arms around the neck of the man while he held her tightly to his body with his hands firmly grasping her buttocks. Rock 'n' roll dancing and jive were also losing popularity. Having successfully withstood attempts to replace them with the cha-cha and the Twist, they had been usurped by the Shake, an unattractive but simple dance in which individuals hopped up and down on the spot while wiggling their hips and waving their arms in the air. The Shake's attraction lay in the fact that not only could it be performed in groups as well as couples but individuals without a partner could also dance it on their own. As I was fanatical about ballroom dancing, rock 'n' roll and jive, I saw these new trends as an unwelcome development.

CHAPTER 18

AN OUT OF DATE ROCK BAND

Despite the many social and leisure activities at the Percy Gee, my student friends and I still found the time to make good use of the music and dance opportunities available in Leicester's city centre. For top class entertainment the venue was the De Montfort Hall, a large concert hall off Regent Road on the edge of Victoria Park, conveniently adjacent to the university campus. Opened in 1913, the 'De Mont', as it was affectionately known to generations of Leicester people, staged popular music performances as well as classical orchestral concerts, and was a regular venue for nationally known jazz bands and rock 'n' roll stars. On Sunday 31 March 1963, The Beatles appeared at the De Montfort with Chris Montez and Tommy Roe. Although it was the Beatles' first visit to the hall, the concert was a sell-out because they were rapidly becoming Britain's top band. Celia managed to obtain a ticket and went to the performance on her own. I declined as I had no intention of attending a rock concert with no dancing. My reticence was justified when Celia complained that she was unable to hear any of the Beatles' music for the screaming of their fans.

In the late 1950s and early 1960s, traditional ballroom dancing remained very popular with young people, despite the growing attractions of jazz, rock 'n' roll and

The De Montfort Hall, Leicester's premier concert venue.

R&B. At the Il Rondo, a small dance hall on Silver Street close to the Clock Tower that was described as being Leicester's contemporary ballroom, it was possible to engage in a different style of dancing every night of the week. On Saturdays, the Kenny Brown Band provided music for modern jive as well as traditional ballroom dancing; on Sundays it was rock 'n' roll; Mondays Jazz and jive; Tuesdays Old Time Dancing, and Fridays were again nights for rocking and rolling. On Mondays, it was the venue for the popular Abracadabra Jazz Club where many national and local bands performed to packed audiences. In reality, my visits to the Il Rondo were few and far between. My preference was for the intimate atmosphere of the Sunday afternoon Club 57 at the Granby Dance Studios, frequently rocking and jiving on the dance floor to student bands and the locally popular Soar Valley Jazz Band. In the early 1960s, jazz was in such demand that it was impossible not to find jazz played somewhere in Leicester every night of the week. Jazz clubs sprang up throughout the city: a Saturday night club at the YMCA on Granby Street; The Original Leicester Jazz Club at various venues including the Bedford Hotel on the Aylestone Road, the Royal Standard on Charles Street and the Victoria on Granby Street; the Casino Jazz Club on London Road; The Standard Bearers Jazz Club at the Barley Mow public house, and the Broken Drum Club at the Pelican. Friday nights were also jazz nights at the White Swan in the Market Place. John reformed his Hot Six in 1963 and became the resident jazz band at the White Swan playing under the name of Das Jazz Kapelle. While traditional jazz had mass appeal, modern jazz had few followers. An attempt by Ronnie Scott to establish modern jazz clubs at the Granby Dance Studios and The Empire Hotel on Fosse Road North were short lived. Leicester was definitely a centre for traditional jazz and the popularity of jazz lasted in the city long after it had waned elsewhere.

Despite its limited appeal, folk music had a small but enthusiastic following. I frequently accompanied Dave Cousins to impromptu folk sessions in various city centre public houses where Dave usually occupied a corner of a bar to sing and play, oblivious of everything happening around him. At the Dover Castle he was billed as 'Dave Cousins and his talking guitar' which was a fairly accurate description of his skills. The Leicester Folk Song Club, established in 1961 by Leicester singers Harvey Tucker, Russ Merryfield and Geoff Halford, was based in an upstairs function room at the Red Cow public house on Belgrave Gate. Every week, dedicated folkies crowded into the function room, beer in hand, to sit on an assorted collection of chairs, stools and couches, or to loll on the floor while listening to the singers. The club was well supported by performers from the university, but especially by Roy Bailey who became the club's unofficial MC. Roy was eventually awarded an MBE in the year 2000 honours list for his services to British folk

★

Contact

J. HODGKINS
40 Evington St.,
Leicester

★

JAZZ

with

JOHN HODGKINS

and

" Das Jazz Kapelle "

with Sue

John Hodgkins' Das Jazz Kapelle.

The Victoria Hotel, Granby Street, a popular location for music and dancing. (by permission of the Record Office for Leicestershire, Leicester and Rutland)

music. During his postgraduate year, Rod developed an interest in traditional blues music and became a regular performer at the Red Cow. While he was staying at 40 Evington Street, Rod joined Celia and me

to form a short-lived folk trio that occasionally performed on club nights at the Red Cow as the Autumn Meadows, a tongue-in-cheek tribute to the popular folk group the Springfields whose music we were copying at the time. We were even paid a small fee for our efforts – a percentage of the door takings, which usually resulted in the grand sum of 2s 6d, that was to be shared equally among the three of us.

For some people, folk music was an expression of their political idealism because it was a major element in the culture of the working classes and, as such, appealed greatly to those of a left-wing persuasion, especially among the student fraternity. In June 1963, Centre 42 organised a festival of culture in Leicester in which folk music

played an important part. During the festival, local singers were encouraged to perform alongside nationally recognised artists that included the Ian Campbell Folk Group, the Spinners, Anne Briggs and the Watersons. Centre 42 was a TUC inspired organisation headed by Arnold Wesker and Ewan MacColl with the aim of promoting arts in the community and working

Rod performing at the Leicester Folk Club in the Red Cow public house.
(R. Davies)

class culture in particular. Not everybody at the university was ready and willing at the time to accept a working class contribution to the world of culture.

> I was invited on Friday evening to attend a concert given by two folk-singers, representatives I gather of the mass movement called cryptically enough (no doubt to avert suspicion) Centre 42. Accordingly I did a bit of gardening in the afternoon to get my trousers dirty, and went along. The audience looked harmless enough, but my suspicions were aroused when I noticed a group of primitive-looking girls wearing boiler suits, and when one of the performers bore on the stage a banjo (a Negro instrument), I prepared myself for the worst. The idea behind this movement is without precedent. Centre 42 labours in the conviction that true culture resides with the working classes and exists in order that we may all partake of it at their public performances.
>
> Leicester Diary, *Ripple*, 25 June 1963

As well as jazz and folk, the early 1960s witnessed a growing demand from young people for rock 'n' roll music. Most of the major dance halls in Leicester devoted at least one night a week to rock 'n' roll with fans dancing to records or local live bands. Every Saturday night at the Granby Dance Studios, young men and women rock 'n' rolled to music from current popular recordings. From 1959, live bands played every week in at least six major dance halls throughout the city and its suburbs: The Il Rondo, The Clarence Ballroom in South Wigston, the Trocadero dance hall on Scraptoft Lane, The Syston Assembly Halls, the Casino on London Road and the Corn Exchange in the market, as well as in the small function rooms of many public houses. Most provided the opportunity for local Leicester groups to be heard, the best of which were the Beatniks, The Rebels, Tony Bart and the Strangers, The Renegades, The Helions and The Saphires, as well as the Incas, the Farinas and Johnny Angel and the Mystics. By 1963, the centre for rock 'n' roll in Leicester was the Il Rondo. As well as local talent, nationally known groups were engaged to perform in front of admiring audiences, challenging the monopoly on big stars previously held by the De Montfort Hall. Among those appearing at the Il Rondo during 1963 were Brian Poole and the Tremeloes, and, in August of that year, the Rolling Stones.

1964 saw an explosion of new clubs in the city offering R&B and rock 'n' roll to audiences of mods and rockers. These included a weekly Rhythm and Blues Rave at Lancaster Hall (a dance venue above the Fire Station on Lancaster Road, close to the university), a Rock and Blues club at a new cellar venue on New Bond Street called The Pitt, and the weekly Two Cities Folk and Blues Club at the Victoria on Granby Street. Once

The Rod Davies Blues Band. (R. Davies)

Rhythm and Blues night at the Victoria Hotel, Granby Street. (R. Davies)

ROD DAVIES BLUES BAND

JAZZ & BLUES CLUB

The Victoria Hotel
Leicester

Membership Card No : 391

Rod Davies Blues Band.

he had passed his Postgraduate Teaching Certificate, Rod formed the Rod Davies Blues Band and enjoyed a few successful years in the mid-60s playing a fusion of blues music with jazz in Leicester's many clubs and colleges, as well as appearing as the regular Saturday evening headline band at the Victoria. The most successful Leicester rock group of 1964 was without doubt the ex-Art and Tech band the Farinas, our long-time friends and college rivals. Had Aztec and the Incas persevered until then, with better equipment and a big dose of luck, they might well have enjoyed a similar successful outcome.

By the summer of 1963, Johnny Angel and the Mystics had become popular outside Leicester and was also appearing at venues throughout the East Midlands, joining the many competent small local groups struggling to become famous. Every fortnight for most of the summer and autumn of that year, we were booked to play at a Saturday dance in a social club in Coalville. Dougie's Elvis impersonation had gone down well with the local girls, who not only surrounded our dressing room to seek out his favours but also screamed incessantly throughout our performances. We were also regular performers at a number of large and impressive working men's clubs in Coventry, most of which were associated with the motor manufacturing industry. Our repertoire of music was now sufficiently strong for the group to play a whole evening of music without repeating any songs. Our stated aim was to add a new musical piece to our repertoire every fortnight and by late summer we had mastered the Shadows' instrumentals *Dance On* and *Foot Tapper*; Kenny Lynch's *Up on the Roof*, Trini Lopez's *If I had a Hammer* and various songs by the emerging new groups from Liverpool including *She Loves You*, *Love Me Do*, and *Please, Please Me* by the Beatles. With much persistence, I also persuaded Alan to take over my bass while I borrowed his Fender guitar to play instrumental versions of *Golden Earrings* and *Hava Nagila*. We also tried to keep up to date by wearing Beatles-style collarless jackets, although Dougie continued to imitate Elvis.

Travelling to our venues was always a problem, especially to out-of-town engagements. In the beginning, Ron and his friend Kevin transported the group and its equipment in their two cars but, as our baggage increased, we needed a van to convey us to our playing locations. Until we were able to purchase a van of our own, we resorted to hiring transport locally. For a time we were driven to our venues in a van owned by an elderly Irishman. Regrettably, he spent most of the time that we were playing in the bar and was often seriously inebriated by the end of the evening. On one occasion when he dropped me at Evington Street, we became involved in an argument with a passing pedestrian who was similarly afflicted and who claimed that our drunken Irish driver had just driven our van over his foot. It soon became clear that a van of our own was a necessity. Not all of our appearances passed without incident. During one performance at Oadby Village Hall a member of the audience began to pay too much attention to Dougie's girlfriend, which provoked him into making a flying leap from the stage to remonstrate with the offender during a Cliff Richard song triggering off a small riot on the dance floor. Unsure as to what might happen next, the rest of the Mystics played on without Dougie. Once proceedings had died down, the dance was cut short and we all made as quick an exit as we could out of the back door in case of possible reprisals.

The pinnacle of the Mystics' achievements came early in 1964 when, in a short period of time, we performed at the Il Rondo, the Casino nightclub, at the Clarence Ballroom in South Wigston (as a supporting band to a new up-and-coming group called The Kinks), in the Students' Union at Loughborough College and were invited to an audition in Birmingham with representatives from ATV with a view to appearing on television.

CORN EXCHANGE.

7.30   TONIGHT   11.45

JOHNNY ANGEL

And

THE MYSTICS

Plus

The Beat Brothers

Advert, *Leicester Mercury*, 9 November 1963

It was during this interview that our shortcomings became apparent. Elvis Presley and Cliff Richard were by now considered middle-of-the-road entertainers, so Dougie's gold lamé suit and white winkle-picker shoes and the synchronised dance steps of the Mystics were considered to be out of date. When we were asked to play a song that we had composed ourselves, the only one that came to mind was our version of the *William Tell Overture*. High kicks did not go down too well with ATV and, consequently, we were never invited to appear on television. It soon became clear to all of us that the style of the Mystics was now old fashioned; promoters were looking for groups with original material, and not bands that played cover versions of other people's music. The discothèque concept was quickly replacing groups like the Mystics. I finally left the band at the end of May 1964, in order to concentrate on my teaching career. Dougie also retired soon after. The Mystics continued playing in Leicester for most of 1964 but eventually reformed under the stage name of Makin Sounds, with Alan as their leader. Alan abandoned his Fender guitar in favour of a newly-fashionable electronic keyboard, introduced a saxophone player and a small brass section and, during the late 1960s, played throughout the Midlands as a blues band in the style of Gino Washington and Otis Redding.

Perhaps more than anything, the end of my days as a rock 'n' roll musician signalled the end of my journey to adulthood, an exciting roller-coaster of a ride that had seen many joyous highs and some desperate lows. I had made mistakes, many of them deeply regretted, but my academic and personal education was now complete. The innocent 18-year-old who began that journey had changed into a somewhat bruised, but more worldly-wise and cautious adult, better able to cope with whatever life might bring. If that was not evidence enough for the end of my journey to manhood then it was in the fact that I sold my bass guitar and amplifier to Rod in July 1964, and for many years thereafter my acoustic guitar and ukulele banjo gradually gathered dust in my spare bedroom before being sold in a jumble sale.

The years between 1958 and 1964 had seen life change for most young people throughout Britain. The arrival of rock 'n' roll music from America in 1956 coincided with the birth of a youth culture; a culture that was characterised for most young men and women by popular music and fashionable clothes. But it also gave a few independent-thinking young people a growing confidence to challenge the social divisions, prejudices and norms of behaviour in contemporary society, although not always for the better; a confidence that was to spawn the revolutionary zeal of the infamous 'swinging sixties' that saw light at the end of the decade, even if the excesses of those times were also restricted to the notorious few. For most ordinary young people, including myself, the effects of those changes on our everyday lifestyles were exciting and dramatic, but maybe not as liberal nor as extreme as popular history tries to suggest.

Yet the educational changes implemented at the end of World War Two had enabled me to gain entry into the world of a university; a world for which I had neither the confidence, understanding nor cultural background needed to make the best of my opportunities. They also enabled me to meet with young people and to embark on relationships with women from vastly different social backgrounds to my own. Perhaps those differences were often so great that it was inevitable such relationships would ultimately fail, and that my most successful and enduring relationship was with Celia, a young woman whose experience and background was similar to my own. Plus ca change, plus c'est la meme chose.

ND - #0290 - 270225 - C0 - 234/156/12 - PB - 9781780910093 - Gloss Lamination